DECODING THE PYRAMIDS

DECODING THE PYRAMIDS

Exploring the world's most enigmatic structures

JOHN DESALVO PHD

METRO BOOKS
NEW YORK

Text © 2008 by John DeSalvo
Design and Layout © 2008 by
Ivy Press Limited

This 2008 edition published by
Metro Books, by arrangement with
the Ivy Press.

This book was conceived,
designed, and produced
by Ixos, an imprint of
Ivy Press
The Old Candlemakers
West Street, Lewes,
East Sussex BN7 2NZ, U.K.

Creative Director Peter Bridgewater
Publisher David Alexander
Editorial Director Caroline Earle
Art Director Sarah Howerd
Design Concept Simon Goggin
Senior Project Editor Mary Todd
Designers John Grain, Kate Haynes
Illustrations Richard Palmer
Picture Research Shelley Noronha,
Katie Greenwood

Metro Books
122 Fifth Avenue
New York, NY 10011

ISBN-13: 978-1-4351-0339-9
ISBN-10: 1-4351-0339-4

Library of Congress Cataloging-in-
Publication data available

Printed and bound in China

10 9 8 7 6 5 4 3 2 1

CONTENTS

FOREWORD
by Dr. Patrick Flanagan

In 1973, I wrote and published the first book ever on pyramid research. I was not sure how it would be received but was very pleased to see it becoming a best seller. Everyone seemed to pick up the term "pyramid power," which was the title of my book. What was so wonderful was that the average person could experiment with this phenomenon in his or her own home, and in fact many people did. A rush of literature and other books followed mine, and the study of the effects of pyramids became worldwide. Even academic researchers and scientists were looking into these unusual phenomena. All sorts of claims were made but my approach was truly scientific. I reported and described specific experimental setups, recording designs, data, and experimental results. Anyone could repeat these experiments with the information I presented.

I always believed, and still believe, that we need to use the scientific method in our approach to this research. We do need to be open to new discoveries but these must be rigorously tested and analyzed. I was lucky in that I had a scientific background.

Many people are aware that I designed the neurophone, which is a device that transmits signals directly to the brain, bypassing the ears and the auditory nerves. Thus, many people with ear and nerve damage could hear sounds through this device. I had also developed a device to detect missile launches anywhere in the world and pinpoint their location and time of launch. Many tell me that the basis of our missile detection system from the 1960s to the 1980s was founded on my design. So I have always had an interest in developing new scientific devices and testing them. I guess I was a "natural" in getting involved in pyramid research. Also, my research into dolphin communication for the military helped me apply some of the studies with neurophysiology to my other interests, including pyramid research.

I am very pleased to write this foreword for my very good friend John DeSalvo, since I am very happy that he is trying to bring together pyramid researchers from all over the world and from many different academic disciplines. His Association is the first to attempt to do this. Dr. DeSalvo also discusses the pyramid research from Russia and the Ukraine, which I have been aware of for a long time and am also actively following. It will be interesting to see what this new research delivers.

I hope you read this book with an open mind and enjoy the diverse theories and opinions that you will encounter. It will give you a good foundation and bring you up to date on all the major theories. Maybe someday your own theory will be added to these.

Patrick Flanagan, M.D., Ph.D., D. Sc., 2007

INTRODUCTION

This book is an illustrated guide and an up-to-date reference source for the Great Pyramid of Giza in Egypt and current pyramid research. It includes the latest discoveries and theories about the Great Pyramid, new scientific breakthroughs into pyramid research, and exclusive photographs of and research within the large contemporary pyramids that have been built in Russia and the Ukraine in the last two decades.

The book incorporates information and diverse research from many of the leading pyramid researchers around the world. In addition, I have relied on numerous sources from the 17th century to the present. In one book, you have access to all this information, and some of the research is published here for the first time.

This book contains one of the most comprehensive tours of the Great Pyramid in print. It includes fascinating stories, quotes from significant historical persons, and the crucial facts about the Great Pyramid. It is up-to-date and brings you the most recent research concerning the Great Pyramid. The sections on its history take you from the time of Herodotus in the 5th century BCE to the present. We look at some interesting subjects along the way, including the possibility of levitation being used in its construction and the earliest legends about the Great Pyramid.

For thousands of years, people have speculated about the purpose of the Great Pyramid. We will look at the major theories, both ancient and modern, and explore the current research in trying to determine the purpose of this structure.

But there are modern pyramids as well, and few people in this country are aware of the gigantic building projects that have been going on in the former Soviet Union. In 1989, Alexander Golod from Moscow, now the Director of a Russian defense enterprise company, started building large fiberglass pyramids, mainly in Russia and the Ukraine. He believed the pyramids produced a unique energy field that has an effect on biological and non-biological materials. To test his theory, over the following ten years he built seventeen large fiberglass pyramids in Russia and the Ukraine. To give you an idea of the size of these pyramids, the largest is 144 ft (44 m) high, weighs over 55 tons (55,880 kg), and cost over 1 million dollars to build.

From 1989 to 1999 the Russian National Academy of Sciences and other leading institutes in Russia and the Ukraine performed many diverse experiments within and around the pyramids, which included studies in medicine, agriculture, ecology, physics, and chemistry. I have been working with Alexander Golod and his son Anatoli, and we have recently formed the International Partnership for Pyramid Research. This is one of the first joint ventures between research groups in the United States and Russia.

Not only has there been a scientific attempt to measure changes in materials produced by pyramids, but also to identify and quantify the energy fields produced by them. Some of this new research has been undertaken by physicists and engineers both in the United States and the former Soviet Union. For the first time, this book will reveal the results of identifying and measuring these newly discovered energy fields. The implications for our future technology will also be discussed.

Pyramid research today is also taking place in the laboratory, using experimental model pyramids and sophisticated scientific apparatus. One person who has spent the last thirty years performing experiments with model pyramids is Joe Parr, one of the Great Pyramid of Giza Research Association's research directors. Joe is an electronics engineer and one of the few people to have spent two entire nights on top of the Great Pyramid conducting scientific measurements. Using rotating pyramids and electromagnetic and radioactive sources, Joe has scientific evidence that under certain conditions strange physical phenomena that operate outside our known laws of physics may occur in pyramids. Many years ago, astronomers discovered a "gamma-ray emitting source" in the center of our galaxy, but to this day no one has yet discovered its cause. Amazingly, there is a correlation between this gamma-ray source and Joe Parr's pyramid experiments. In addition to Joe's research, we will discuss other pyramid experiments that are taking place in different laboratories around the world today.

In the 1970s, the term "pyramid power" implied that some unknown force was at work in pyramids that could preserve food, sharpen razor blades, and help people to meditate. The first book ever published on pyramid power was by Dr. Patrick Flanagan in 1973. His pioneering work set the stage for future research and scientific studies. We may have discovered the scientific basis for this force, and we will discuss this research and its findings in this book for the first time.

This book contains resources not readily available to the general public because much of the information comes from books that are out of print or very difficult to find. Also included is one of the most extensive bibliographies in print about the Great Pyramid and other pyramid research published since the 17th century.

Most books on the Great Pyramid espouse the theories and viewpoints of the author. This book is objective in that it does not promote any one theory or viewpoint but presents all the major theories in an objective way. In that sense, there is no other book like it.

I invite you to begin your tour of the Great Pyramid of Giza.

THE GREAT PYRAMID

"The Great Pyramid of Giza was originally covered with beautiful polished limestone."

CHAPTER ONE

THE STAR ON EARTH

The Great Pyramid of Giza was originally covered with beautiful polished limestone, known as casing stone. The ancient Greek writer Strabo is quoted as saying: "It seemed like a building let down from heaven, untouched by human hands." It has been calculated that the original pyramid with its casing stones would have acted like a gigantic mirror, reflecting light so powerful that it would be visible from the moon as a shining star on Earth.

The Great Pyramid of Giza is the sole surviving and oldest of the seven wonders of the ancient world. It is situated 10 miles (16 km) west of Cairo, on the west bank of the Nile, on the northern edge of the Giza Plateau, which covers 1 square mile (2.6 km²).

MASSIVE DIMENSIONS

It has been estimated to be composed of over 2½ million blocks of limestone, which weigh between 2 and 70 tons each. Recent quarry evidence indicates that there may only be about 750,000 blocks, weighing between ½ and 2 tons each. As nobody knows for sure what the interior of the pyramid is like, these calculations are based on assumptions. Its base covers over 13 acres (5 hect) and its volume is approximately 90 million cu ft (27.4 million m³). You could build over thirty Empire State Buildings with its masonry. It originally rose to a height of 484 ft (147.5 m), though it is now about 454 ft (138 m) high, the equivalent to a modern fifty-storey building. There are currently 203 courses, or steps, to its summit and the four triangular sides each slope upward at an angle of about 52 degrees (more precisely, 51 degrees 50 min 40 sec).

Most Perfect Masonry

In his *Illustrated Handbook of Architecture*, 1855, James Ferguson writes of "the most perfect and gigantic specimen of masonry that the world has yet seen. No one can possibly examine the interior of the Great Pyramid without being struck with astonishment at the wonderful mechanical skill displayed in its construction."

PREVIOUS PAGE
The three main pyramids on
the Giza Plateau: The Great
Pyramid, Chephren's Pyramid,
and Menkaure's Pyramid.

RIGHT
The Great Pyramid of Giza,
seen here at night lit up by
spotlights, rises to a height
of 454 ft (138 m). This is
equivalent to a modern
fifty-storey building.

BELOW
This is the only statue or
representation of Pharaoh
Khufu known to exist. It
is about 3 in (7.6 cm) high,
made of ivory, and is
displayed in the Cairo
Museum. It was thought
that the Great Pyramid
was built during
Khufu's reign, but
many researchers
now believe it is
much older.

The joints between adjacent blocks fit together
with optical precision and less than $1/50$ of an
inch (0.508 cm) separates individual blocks. The
cement that was used is extremely fine and strong
and defies chemical analysis. It also appears that,
if pressure is applied, the blocks will break before
the cemented joints. Today, with all our modern
science and engineering, we could not build a
pyramid like the Great Pyramid of Giza.

ORIENTATION & DATING

The pyramid is oriented to true north with
a greater accuracy than any monument,
astronomical site, or any other known
building in the world. Today, the most
accurate north-oriented structure is the
Paris Observatory, which is 6 minutes
of a degree off true north. The Great
Pyramid of Giza is only 3 minutes of a
degree off true north. Studies have shown
that this may be due to either a shift in
the Earth's pole or movement of the
African continent. Thus, when first built, the Great
Pyramid may have been perfectly oriented.

Most Egyptologists claim that the Great Pyramid
was constructed around 2550 BCE, during the reign
of Khufu (known to the Greeks as Cheops) in the
4th Dynasty (2575–2465 BCE). The only known
statue or representation of Khufu to exist is a 3 in
(7.6 cm) ivory statue in the Cairo Museum.

Others researchers question this date, since
erosion studies on the Giza Plateau indicate
that the Great Pyramid is much older. In fact,
some researchers have proposed that the Great
Pyramid may be thousands of years older than
the currently accepted date. Either way, it was
the most magnificent structure in the ancient
world. There is no comparison between the Great
Pyramid of Giza and the other ancient pyramids
of Egypt. The workmanship is far superior and
the precise, elaborate interior structure is unique
among pyramids. Since it does not fit in with any
of these other pyramids, it appears to have come
out of nowhere.

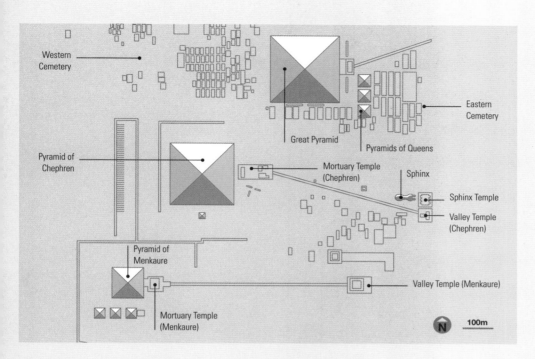

Western
Cemetery

Great Pyramid

Eastern
Cemetery

Pyramids of Queens

Pyramid of
Chephren

Mortuary Temple
(Chephren)

Sphinx

Sphinx Temple

Valley Temple
(Chephren)

Pyramid of
Menkaure

Valley Temple (Menkaure)

Mortuary Temple
(Menkaure)

N   100m

LEFT

Map of the Giza Plateau
showing the three pyramids,
the Great Pyramid of Giza
(the largest), Chephren's
Pyramid (the second largest),
and Menkaure's Pyramid
(the smallest).

NEIGHBORING PYRAMIDS

Next to the Great Pyramid stand two more large pyramids. Academic Egyptologists attribute the slightly smaller one (471 ft/143.5 m high) to Khufu's son and successor, Chephren (Khafra). It still has its uppermost casing stones intact. The other, much smaller (213 ft/65 m high), with its bottom courses sheathed in red granite, is traditionally attributed to Chephren's successor, the grandson of Khufu, Mykerinus (Menkaure).

Visibly, it appears that the second pyramid (Chephren's) is larger than the Great Pyramid. Chephren's Pyramid is 471 ft (143.5 m) high. However, the Great Pyramid with its original capstone would have reached 484 ft (147.5 m). Therefore, in its original state it would have been about 13 ft (4 m) higher than Chephren's Pyramid. However, without its capstone the Great Pyramid is 454 ft (138.3 m); that is 17 ft (5 m) lower than Chephren's. Also, Chephren's pyramid is built on higher ground; about 30 ft (9 m) higher than the ground on which the Great Pyramid is built.

LAND OF PYRAMIDS

The debate goes on concerning who built these pyramids, and when and how they were built. The total number of identifiable pyramids in Egypt is about 100, all of which are built on the west side of the Nile. In addition to the three main Giza pyramids, there are seven smaller or subsidiary ones on the Giza Plateau that are attributed to Khufu's family members.

Pyramid Damage

The damage done to the Great Pyramid by man is an unfortunate consequence of history. Besides the casing stones being stripped in the 14th century by the Arabs to build mosques and other buildings, explorers have also left their marks. In his explorations of the 1830s, Colonel Vyse used gunpowder to try to find hidden entrances and chambers. A huge and ugly 30-ft (9-m) scar made in his attempt to find a hidden entrance on the south side of the Great Pyramid is highly visible today.

But remember, the finished pyramid was covered with casing stones and this effect would not have been produced. No one knows why this precise indentation was built into each side knowing that the pyramid would be finally covered with casing stones. It is very interesting that Petrie found no evidence of this hollowing on the lower casing stones that were still intact.

While looking up at the Great Pyramid, you may be tempted to climb right up to its summit. It is a long and hard climb and would take about an hour with several stops to rest along the way.

ABOVE
The Sphinx today is highly eroded. One of the largest man-made statues in existence, who or what it depicts remains a mystery.

RIGHT
The pyramidion (capstone) of Pharaoh Amenemhat III of the 12th Dynasty. Pyramidions were made with materials such as gold or polished stone and were highly decorated.

SHADOW MYSTERY

A very interesting and often overlooked feature of the Great Pyramid is that its four faces are slightly concave, which is not apparent to the naked eye. Sir William Flinders Petrie noted this hollowing on each face of the pyramid in 1883. On the northern face, it was as much as 37 in (94 cm). This effect is only visible from the air and under certain lighting conditions and lines of sight. Because of this hollowing, a shadow appears at dawn and sunset on the equinoxes on the southern face of the Great Pyramid.

Many tourists in the past have reached the top of the pyramid, but today guards will try to stop you climbing up since some people have fallen to their deaths in this pursuit.

CAPSTONES

The Great Pyramid is flat-topped and not pointed, which a pyramid should be. Its apex, or capstone, seems to be missing. In 1874, a large steel mast was erected on the summit by two astronomers, David Gill and Professor Watson, to mark the position of the apex of the pyramid as it originally would have been. This mast is still there today.

When a pyramid was constructed, the top part, or capstone, was usually the last item to be put in place. The remains of a pyramidion (the capstone) were discovered on the Giza Plateau in the 1980s, and had probably come from one of the small satellite pyramids. The capstone was considered the most important part of the pyramid and was made of special polished stone, or even gold, and highly decorated.

Whether the Great Pyramid was intentionally built without a capstone, or was never completed, or whether the capstone was stolen or destroyed, is unknown. But the accounts of visitors to the pyramid from the ancient past (as far back as the time of Christ) always noted that the pyramid lacked a capstone.

Capstones made of gold or other valuable metals were probably the first items to be looted. However, in this case, the capstone would have been very large and hard to remove. If you climbed to the top, you could walk around very freely on the pyramid's flat surface, as many have done; it is about 20 ft² (6 m²). Thus, this capstone would have been huge and weighed a tremendous amount. No one has been able to explain why the Great Pyramid would have been built without a capstone, if indeed it was.

LEFT
This large steel mast on top of the Great Pyramid was placed there by astronomers David Gill and Professor Watson in 1874 to show where the apex of the pyramid would be if it was finished, or if a capstone was placed upon it.

The Missing Capstone

One of the earliest references to the missing capstone of the Great Pyramid is from the Greek writer Diodorus Siculus in 60 BCE. He says that in his day, when the pyramid stood with its casing stones intact, the structure was, "complete and without the least decay, and yet it lacked its apex stone."

BELOW
This aerial view of the Great Pyramid shows its flat top where the missing capstone would have been. If you climb to the top, it is possible to walk around quite freely on the surface.

ELECTROSTATIC PHENOMENA

Many tourists have climbed to the top of the Great Pyramid. One such person, Sir William Siemens, climbed to the top with his Arab guides at the end of the 19th century. One of Sir Siemens's guides discovered that when he raised his hand with fingers spread apart, he could hear a ringing noise. When Siemens raised his index finger, he felt a prickling sensation. He also received an electric shock when he tried to drink from a bottle of wine. As an experiment, Siemens moistened a newspaper and wrapped it around the wine bottle to convert it into a Leyden Jar (an early form of capacitor). When he held it above his head, it became charged with electricity and sparks were emitted from the bottle. This is a very interesting phenomenon; it appears that there is a high electrostatic charge at the top of the pyramid.

SOLVING THE PUZZLE

It's safe to say that we have been seeking an answer to the riddle of the Great Pyramid for over 4,000 years. Why was it built? Theories range from a tomb or monument for a Pharaoh; an astronomical observatory; a place for elaborate Egyptian rituals; a giant sundial; a grain storage structure; a prophetic monument; a water irrigation system; a repository for ancient knowledge; the Egyptian *Book of the Dead* (the world's earliest spiritual literature, over 3,500 years old) immortalized in stone; or perhaps a communication device to other worlds or realms. The question of who actually

built the Great Pyramid and when still remains a mystery. A possible list of builders includes the ancient Egyptians, people from the legendary Atlantis, the Biblical patriarchs Seth or Enoch, and of course extra-terrestrials, to name a few.

UNIQUE & INTRICATE

What makes the Great Pyramid of Giza so unique is that it is the only known pyramid to have a magnificent internal system. Before the Great Pyramid came into existence, such a peculiar internal construction was unknown. From what we can deduce, all subsequent pyramids were poor imitations and did not approach the magnificence of the Great Pyramid.

If the Great Pyramid was originally built as a tomb or a monument for a Pharaoh, why did the builders take the time and trouble to construct such an intricate internal structure? The mathematician E. Licks states: "So mighty is the Great Pyramid

at Gizeh and so solidly is it constructed that it will undoubtedly remain standing long after all other buildings now on Earth have disappeared," (*Recreations in Mathematics*, 1917).

The Seven Wonders of the Ancient World

Philo of Byzantium compiled the list of the Seven Wonders of the Ancient World in the second century BCE. The Great Pyramid of Giza was named as the First Wonder of the Ancient World, and it is the only one still remaining. The other Wonders were: the Colossus of Rhodes; the Statue of Zeus at Olympia; the Mausoleum at Halicarnassus; the Hanging Gardens of Babylon; the Temple of Artemis (Diana) at Ephesus; and the Lighthouse of Alexandria.

SHINING LIKE A JEWEL

The casing stones that originally covered the pyramid came from the quarries of Tura and Masara in the Moqattam Hills on the opposite side of the Nile. These casing stones reflected the sun's light and made the pyramid shine like a jewel. The ancient Egyptians called the Great Pyramid "Ikhet," meaning the "Glorious Light."

Today, only a few of these are left in position, on each side at the base. The Arabs stripped off most of them in the 14th century after an earthquake loosened many. They used them to build mosques and buildings in Cairo. One of the largest remaining casing stones is nearly 5 ft (1.5 m) high by 8 ft (2.4 m) and weighs about 15 tons. How these blocks were transported and assembled remains a mystery. To manufacture just two blocks with a tolerance of 0.010 in/0.0254 cm (the permissible limit of variation in machining) and place them together with a gap of no more than 0.020 in (0.508 cm) is a remarkable feat. The Great Pyramid had at one time over 100,000 similar casing stones. This kind of precision in the ancient world is unheard of. How could a primitive society build a structure that is so accurate without advanced technology at its disposal?

It has been calculated that the casing stones of the original pyramid would have turned it into a gigantic mirror and reflected light so powerful that it would have been visible from the moon as a shining star on earth.

In 1837 Colonel Howard Vyse, after seven months of work with over a hundred assistants, and at enormous expense, brought the Great Pyramid within the sphere of modern scientific investigation. When Vyse cleared away some debris by the pyramid, he discovered two of the original polished limestone casing stones.

ABOVE
When first completed, the entire pyramid was covered with smooth, highly polished limestone blocks known as casing stones, some of which are still visible at the base of the north end of the pyramid.

FAR LEFT
A view of Chephren's pyramid showing the original casing stones still intact at the top.

CHAPTER TWO

THE GRAND GALLERY

The Great Pyramid has been explored by many people throughout history, and many of them have added to our understanding of the pyramid. We begin with the most famous exploration by an Arab Caliph, Abdullah Al Mamoun, in the ninth century. His motivation was to find treasure within the Great Pyramid.

In 820 CE, under Caliph Abdullah Al Mamoun, the Arabs searched for a secret entrance into the Great Pyramid, but they did not find one. His workmen then attempted to burrow straight into the solid rock of the pyramid in the hope of finding a passage. They tunneled over 100 ft (30 m) into the solid core of the pyramid, and were about to give up when they heard the sound of something falling to the east of the tunnel. They altered their direction toward the sound and eventually broke into the Descending Passage. The workers stated that it was, "exceedingly dark, dreadful to look at, and difficult to pass."

INSIDE THE PYRAMID

They discovered that the Great Pyramid has two systems of passages, a downward, or descending, system and an upward, or ascending, system. The entry into the pyramid is on the north side, about 56 ft (17 m) above ground level. The passages are all on the same vertical plane, parallel to the north–south axis of the pyramid. They are not in the direct center of the pyramid but off by 24 ft (7 m) to the east of center. Thus the entrance to the pyramid is not on the centerline of the north side, but to the east of it by 24 ft (7 m). Also, all chambers extend westward from the vertical plane of the passage system, and none extend eastward.

A Hinged Door

Strabo, a Greek geographer, visited the pyramids in 24 BCE. He describes an entrance on the north face of the pyramid made of a hinged stone which could be raised but which was indistinguishable from the surrounding stone when closed. The location of this moveable door was lost during the first century CE.

THE WAY IN

The original entrance, created by the builders of the Great Pyramid, leads to the descending passage, which slopes down at an angle of 26 degrees and measures 3½ ft (1.06 m) wide by almost 4 ft (1.2 m) high. The distance from this passage to the beginning of the horizontal Subterranean Chamber passage is 344 ft (104.8 m).

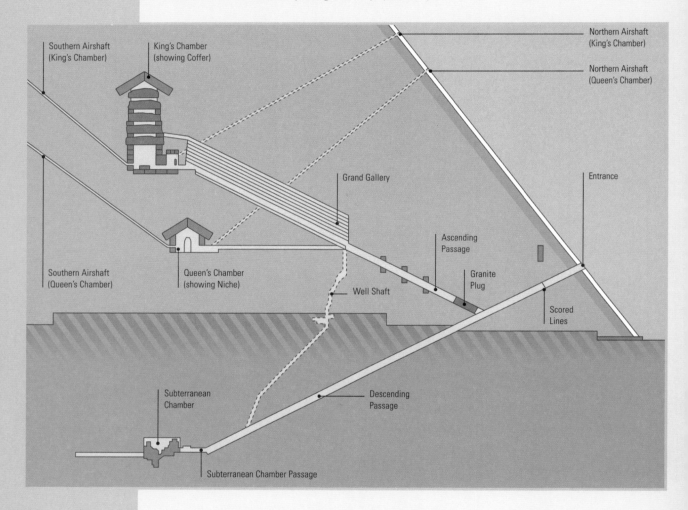

Southern Airshaft
(King's Chamber)

King's Chamber
(showing Coffer)

Northern Airshaft
(King's Chamber)

Northern Airshaft
(Queen's Chamber)

Grand Gallery

Entrance

Ascending
Passage

Southern Airshaft
(Queen's Chamber)

Queen's Chamber
(showing Niche)

Granite
Plug

Well Shaft

Scored
Lines

Subterranean
Chamber

Descending
Passage

Subterranean Chamber Passage

About 40 ft (105 m) down from the original entrance, there appear to be scored lines running along both sides of the Descending Passage. Some have suggested that they signify a starting point in the Great Pyramid. The scored lines are of high precision, but their significance remains a mystery. There is a granite plug in the ceiling 97 ft (29.5 m) down the Descending Passage, which blocks the entrance to the Ascending Passage. The plug is made of very hard quartz, mica, and feldspar. It is actually composed of three granite plugs side by side.

Al Mamoun's workmen dug around these plugs through the softer limestone to gain entrance into the Ascending Passage. Once clear, they forced their way into the Ascending Passage. Moving upwards, they found themselves in the Grand Gallery, and from there explored the Queen's Chamber and the King's Chamber. The men searched everywhere for treasure, but the only thing they found was a large lidless coffin of highly polished granite. Arab legend says that in this coffin they found a stone statue with sword, breastplate of gold with precious gems, and a large ruby on the head, which gave off light. It is said that the statue was inscribed with strange writing that no one could translate.

THE PASSAGES

The Ascending Passage slopes up at a 26-degree angle (the same angle as the Descending Passage slopes down) and has the same dimensions as the Descending Passage (4 ft/1.2 m high by almost 3½ ft/1.06 m wide).

A Swivel Door

Many researchers think that the Great Pyramid was built with a swivel door at its entrance. It would have weighed about 20 tons and been balanced so that it could be opened by pushing on it from the inside. When closed, it would form a perfect fit that could not be detected. Swivel doors have been found in just two other pyramids: those built by Sneferu and Huni, Khufu's father and grandfather respectively.

Due to the lack of height in the Ascending Passage, you would have to stoop as you climbed upward at an incline of 26 degrees. This would become very tiring.

THE GRAND GALLERY

BELOW
The north end of the Grand Gallery. Notice the two narrow ramps on either side that are slotted at regular intervals.

BELOW RIGHT
A painting of Arab explorers entering the Grand Gallery of the Great Pyramid.

Following the Ascending Passage for 124 ft (38 m), Al Mamoun's workmen finally arrived at a large open space now known as the Grand Gallery. At this point of intersection, there are two routes: you can continue going up the Grand Gallery and eventually reach the King's Chamber, or you can carry on in a horizontal direction through another passage (127 ft/39 m long) and wind up in the Queen's Chamber. We will first continue through the Grand Gallery to the King's Chamber. Also at this intersection (where the Ascending Passage meets with the Grand Gallery) is a hole that leads to a shaft (known as the Well Shaft), which connects with the Descending Passage below. This near-vertical tunnel is about 3 ft (1 m) in diameter.

The Grand Gallery is about 26 ft (7.9 m) high, 7 ft (2.1 m) wide at the floor level (including the ramps on each side) and 153 ft (46.6 m) long. It continues upward at the same slope as the Ascending Passage. The walls rise in seven courses of polished limestone, each corbeled 3 in (7.6 cm) toward the center, making the gallery narrow from 7 ft (2.1 m) at the base to 41 in (1.4 m) at the top. The ramps are about 20 in (0.5 m) wide.

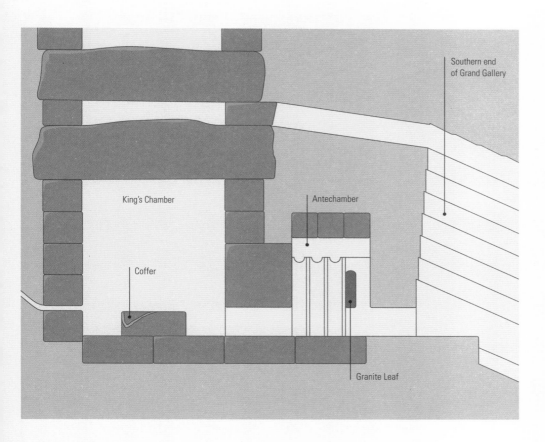

THE GREAT STEP

At the top of the Grand Gallery lies a huge stone step, which measures 6 ft (1.8 m) wide by 3 ft (1 m) high. It forms a platform 8 ft (2.4 m) deep, which is very worn and chipped, and has been referred to as the "Great Step." Past the Great Step is another low, horizontal passage 41 in² (104 cm²), which leads to the King's Chamber. A third of the way along this passage, it rises and widens into a sort of Antechamber; the south, east, and west walls of this passage are no longer limestone but red granite.

ENTERING THE ANTECHAMBER

At the top of the Great Step, you need to bow down to enter the low square passage, which is only 3 ½ ft (1.1 m) high, to enter the Antechamber. After going forward about 4 ft (1.2 m), you enter the Antechamber and can stand up in a little compartment measuring 21 in (64 cm) from front to back and 41 in (104 cm) from side to side.

A suspended stone slab, also known as the "Granite Leaf," appears in front of you. It is nearly 16 in (40.6 cm) thick and composed of two blocks, one on top of the other. They are fitted into grooves in the wall. This slab only descends to the level of the roof of the entrance passageway, so you need to duck under this slab to continue. Once you exit the antechamber, you enter another low passage that continues for about 8 ft (2.4 m) until you enter the King's Chamber. To many, the King's Chamber is the most important, sacred, and mysterious part of the Great Pyramid. It does appear to be the central part of this pyramid and we will now explore further this most interesting and enigmatic chamber.

ABOVE LEFT

Cross section showing the King's Chamber, Antechamber, and south end of the Grand Gallery. Areas shaded in red are composed of granite.

ABOVE

The "Granite leaf" is a suspended stone slab in the Antechamber. It is almost 16 in (40.6 cm) thick and composed of two blocks, one on top of the other.

CHAPTER THREE

THE KING'S CHAMBER

The King's Chamber is one of the most intriguing parts of the Great Pyramid. There has been more speculation about its purpose and use than of any other chamber in the pyramid. This is the place that most visitors to the Great Pyramid want to explore and experience. Indeed, Alexander the Great was said to have spent time in the King's Chamber, and Napoleon certainly did too.

The King's Chamber is constructed entirely out of granite. Its dimensions are approximately 19 ft (5.7 m) high with a floor area of 34 ft by 17 ft (10.3 m by 5 m). There are exactly 100 blocks making up the walls of the King's Chamber. The granite is red (composed of granules of quartz, feldspar, and mica) and comes from the quarries at Aswan (Syene), which is about 500 miles (800 km) from Giza. The roof is formed of enormous granite beams (one of the largest weighs about 70 tons). The Coffer, located in the King's Chamber, is the only artifact known to be found in the Great Pyramid (besides the small artifacts found in the airshafts in the Queen's Chamber; see Chapter 5). The Coffer is a lidless box cut from a solid block of granite that measures 6 ½ ft (2 m) long, 2 ¼ ft (0.7 m) wide, and 3 ft (1 m) deep. It may have once had a sliding lid because there is a ridge along the top edge of the Coffer. The Coffer is chipped at one of its corners.

As well as being known as the Coffer, the box is also sometimes referred to as the Coffin, the Sarcophagus, the Granite Box, and the Empty Stone Chest, amongst other names. It is currently located a few yards away from the west wall of the chamber, but many think it was originally located in the center. Also, because it is too large to pass through the low passages leading into the King's Chamber, it must have been placed in the chamber before it was closed and the passages sealed. Researchers who dispute that the Great Pyramid was built as a tomb also rule out that this box was used as a coffin. Thus, they prefer the name Coffer to Sarcophagus or Coffin, but can offer no explanation as to its function.

ABOVE

The Battle of the Pyramids—
between the French army
in Egypt under Napoleon
and the local ruling Mamluk
forces—took place on July
21, 1798, only 9 miles (14.5
km) from the Giza pyramids.
Napoleon said to his forces,
"Remember that from those
monuments forty centuries
look down upon you."

PREVIOUS PAGE

The Coffer in the King's
Chamber is made entirely
out of granite.

THEORIES ABOUT THE COFFER

Many interesting things have been reported about the Coffer since the 17th century. In 1646, John Greaves, a British mathematician, astronomer, and explorer, described the Coffer in the earliest known scientific publication on the Great Pyramid. In the following excerpt, the "Room" he refers to is the King's Chamber and the "Monument" is the Coffer:

"Within this glorious Room (for so I may justly call it), as within some consecrated Oratory, stands the Monument of Cheops, or Chemmis, of one piece of Marble, hollow within and uncovered at the top, and sounding like a Bell… This monument, in respect of the nature and quality of the Stone, is the same with which the whole Room is lined; as by breaking a little fragment of it, I plainly discovered, being a speckled kind of Marble, with black, and white, and red Spots, as it were equally mix'd, which some Writers call The baick Marble."

In 1715, Père Claude Sicard visited the Great Pyramid. His account is interesting in that, like Greaves, he also describes an unusual feature of the Coffer in the King's Chamber. He states:

"It was formed out of a single block of granite, had no cover, and when struck, sounded like a bell." Several other explorers of the Great Pyramid have also noted the strange melodic sound that the Coffer emits when struck.

In 1753, Abbé Claude-Louis Fourmont visited the Great Pyramid and noted that the sonorous coffin had no inscription on it.

NAPOLEON'S VISIT

After Napoleon invaded Egypt in 1798, he visited the Great Pyramid and asked to be left alone in the King's Chamber. When he emerged, it was reported that he looked visibly shaken. When an aide asked him whether he had witnessed anything mysterious, he replied that he had no comment, and that he never wanted the incident mentioned again. In 1821, when he was on his deathbed, a close friend asked him what really happened in the King's Chamber. He was about to tell him but stopped, shook his head and said, "No, what's the use. You'd never believe me." As far as we know, he never told anyone and took the secret to his grave. There is, however, an unsubstantiated story that Napoleon had hinted that he was given some vision of his destiny during his stay in the King's Chamber.

Many people who have visited and studied the Great Pyramid feel that the King's Chamber is the most sacred place in the pyramid. Strange phenomena reportedly happen there, such as out-of-body experiences, manifestations of strange lights and orbs, visions, noises, and other paranormal experiences.

The Coffer

This beautiful granite box, often called the Coffer, is made from a solid block of chocolate-colored granite. It appears to be made from an even harder and darker red granite than that making up the walls, floor, and ceilings of the chamber.

Ancient Technology

William Flinders Petrie was one of the first to do extensive scientific excavations in Egypt and the Giza Plateau in the 1880s. In his 1880 exploration of the pyramid, he thought that the Coffer had been fashioned using jewel-tipped saws and drills. In fact, he said, "Truth to tell, modern drill cores cannot hold a candle to the Egyptians." Was he hinting at an unknown technology that the Egyptians had at their disposal?

BELOW

Illustration showing the Grand Gallery being examined by Napoleon's men during an expedition to the Great Pyramid in 1799.

THE AIRSHAFTS

In the King's Chamber on opposite ends of the north and south walls are openings called airshafts. These were discovered by Colonel Vyse in 1837. The shafts are about 9 in² (23 cm²) and extend over 200 ft (60 m). They exit to the outside of

the pyramid. The purpose of these shafts remains a mystery but one possibility is that they were created to bring fresh air into the chamber. John Greaves, in his 1638 visit, thought that these openings were receptacles for lamps.

There is an interesting story associated with the discovery of these shafts. After Colonel Vyse had made the discovery, he wanted to find out whether the shafts led to the outside. One of his assistants, a Mr. Hill, climbed up onto the outer surface of the pyramid and found similar openings where the airshafts exited. Another of Vyse's engineers, called Perring, was in the King's Chamber at the time. Hill, on the outside of the airshaft, accidentally dislodged a stone which came down the 200 ft (60 m) long airshaft at high speed, almost injuring Perring.

When the airshafts were cleaned and opened by Vyse, cool air immediately entered the King's Chamber. Since that time, the King's Chamber has always maintained a constant comfortable temperature of 68°F (20°C), no matter what the temperature outside. This seems to be one of the earliest forms of air conditioning.

THE IRON PLATE

Vyse also discovered a flat iron plate, 12 in by 4 in (30 cm by 10 cm) and ⅛ in (0.064 cm) thick. This plate was removed from a joint in the masonry at the place where the Southern Airshaft of the King's Chamber exits to the outside. Experts conclude that it was left in the joint during the building of the pyramid and could not have been inserted afterwards. This is highly significant, because the date for the Iron Age in Egypt is around 650 BCE and the traditionally accepted date for the building of the pyramid is 2500 BCE. Vyse's discovery is explored in detail in Chapter 5.

THE RELIEVING CHAMBER

When Al Mamoun broke into the pyramid in the ninth century, he ordered his workmen to dig up the floor in the King's Chamber close to the Coffer to look for hidden passageways. He also dug a small hole under the Coffer itself. Vyse had his workers enlarge the hole made by Al Mamoun. He also found nothing. Above the roof of the King's Chamber a series of five cavities, or chambers, have been found. These have been labeled "relieving chambers" by Egyptologists since they think that the purpose of these spaces was to prevent the collapse of the King's Chamber from the

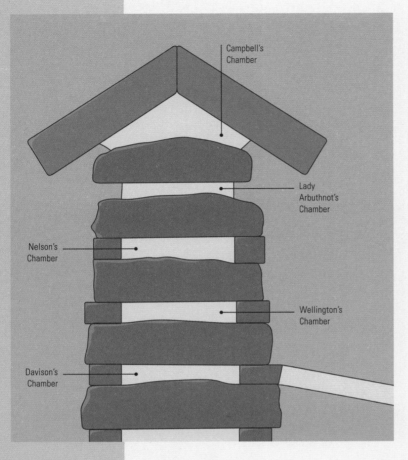

Campbell's Chamber

Lady Arbuthnot's Chamber

Nelson's Chamber

Wellington's Chamber

Davison's Chamber

raised it up, and noticed at the top of the Grand Gallery a small rectangular hole about 2 ft (0.6 m) wide. He put seven ladders together to climb to the top and found 16 in (40.6 cm) of bat dung in the hole. Davison put a kerchief over his face and made his way into the hole. After crawling 25 ft (7.6 m), he reached a chamber about 3 ft (1 m) high but as wide and as long as the King's Chamber beneath. He observed that the floor consisted of the tops of nine rough granite slabs, each weighing as much as 70 tons. The ceiling of the King's Chamber was formed by the undersides of these blocks. He also noticed the ceiling of this relieving chamber was constructed of a similar row of granite blocks. This is as far as he went. This chamber, known as "Davison's Chamber," was named after him. His measurements also confirmed the fact that the pyramid was constructed so that its sides faced the cardinal points of a compass.

FURTHER CHAMBERS

Colonel Vyse also discovered four other chambers above Davison's Chamber. When he found a crack in the ceiling in Davison's Chamber, he decided to run a reed through it. It went through for about 3 ft (1 m) before it stopped. Suspecting another chamber above Davison's, Vyse tried to chisel through the granite overhead but it was too hard. Special quarrymen were brought in but even they could not break through the hard granite. Eventually, gunpowder was used to blast into the upper chamber. This was very dangerous because the blasted granite flew like shrapnel. Vyse named the new chamber (above Davison's) Wellington's Chamber. He also discovered three more chambers above these two, making a total of five chambers above the King's Chamber. From lowest to highest, the chambers

tremendous weight of the masonry above the chamber area which amounts to several million tons. This explanation has recently been questioned, and the purpose of these chambers is still being debated.

DAVISON'S CHAMBER

Nathaniel Davison, British Consul at Algiers in 1763, discovered the lowest of the relieving chambers. He noticed that his voice was echoed in a strange way when he was at the top end of the Grand Gallery. It seemed to resonate from above. Davison tied a candle to the end of two long canes, are Davison's, Wellington's, Nelson's, Lady Arbuthnot's, and Campbell's Chamber, all named by Vyse in honor of dignitaries. This excavation took him almost four months to complete. He published his work in 1837 under the title *Operations Carried on at the Pyramid of Gizeh.*

While exploring these chambers, Vyse apparently came across the cartouches (hieroglyphics of the royal names of Pharaohs enclosed in an oval) of Khufu and his brother Chephren, as co-regent with him, in the form of mason's marks, painted in red ocher on the ceiling beams. Many researchers have questioned this discovery in recent years. From studying the diary of Vyse and careful analysis of the hieroglyphics, some have accused Vyse of painting the cartouches himself in order to be known as the person who proved Khufu built the Great Pyramid. The evidence used is that the spelling of "Khufu" on the blocks is different to the way that scholars of that time believed the name should have been spelled. On the other hand, it is known that the Egyptian pharaohs used several different names for different purposes. Therefore it was not unusual for a pharaoh to have up to half a dozen names, each with a different spelling. The debate over whether these marks were forged by Vyse or are original quarry marks continues.

Caviglia in Residence

In 1817 an Italian seaman and merchant, Captain Caviglia, was enthralled by the mystery of the Great Pyramid and decided to give up seafaring to explore it. Believe it or not, Caviglia cleaned out the bat dung from Davison's Chamber and turned it into an apartment in which he resided.

CHAPTER FOUR

THE QUEEN'S CHAMBER

The Queen's Chamber is rectangular and made from limestone blocks. The floor is composed of rough stone and may never have been finished. The first explorers to enter this chamber noted that its walls were encrusted with salt, but where this came from remains a mystery. No salt remains today as the Chamber has since been cleaned.

A s mentioned before, if you continue at the junction of the Ascending Passage and the Grand Gallery, through the horizontal passage, you reach the Queen's Chamber, which is directly beneath the apex of the pyramid. This passage is 3 ft 9 in (1.1 m) high and 3 ft 5 in (1.04 m) wide. A sudden drop of 2 ft (0.6 m) occurs towards the end of the passage before the entrance to the Queen's Chamber. The chamber has a rough floor and a gabled limestone roof. The name "Queen's Chamber" is a misnomer. The Arab custom was to place women in tombs with gabled ceilings (as opposed to flat ones for men), so this room came to be known by the Arabs as the Queen's Chamber. The floor area of the chamber is 18 ft 10 in by 17 ft 2 in (5.7 m by 4.9 m). It has a double-pitched ceiling, 20 ft 6 in (6.2 meters) at its highest point, formed by huge blocks of limestone at a slope of about 30 degrees. When this chamber was first entered, the walls were encrusted with salt up to ½ in (1.27 cm) thick. This has been removed since then, most likely when the chamber was cleaned. Salt encrustation was also found on the walls of the Subterranean Chamber, the cause of which is also unknown.

THE EMPTY GRANITE BOX

There is a report by an Arab, Edrisi, who died around 1166 CE. He entered the pyramid through the forced entrance made by Al Mamoun and describes not only an empty granite box (the Coffer) in the King's Chamber, but also a similar one in the Queen's Chamber. It was uninscribed and undecorated, just like the one in the King's Chamber. Whatever happened to this granite box in the Queen's Chamber, if it ever existed, remains a mystery.

THE QUEEN'S CHAMBER AIRSHAFTS

We have seen that the airshafts from the King's Chamber exited on the outside of the pyramid (see page 32). It appears that the Queen's Chamber airshafts do not lead to the outside but may terminate within the pyramid.

ABOVE
The Descending Passage slopes down at 26 degrees, the same angle that the Ascending Passage slopes upward. It also has roughly the same dimensions as the Ascending Passage, being 4 ft (1.2 m) high by 3½ ft (1 m) wide.

PREVIOUS PAGE
The Niche inside the Queen's Chamber. It is just over 16 ft (5 m) high, and was originally 3½ ft (1 m) deep.

These airshafts were discovered in 1872 by British engineer Waynman Dixon and his brother, John. A crack was observed in the south wall of the Queen's Chamber in a spot where they suspected an airshaft might be located. They inserted a wire into this crack and it went through a certain distance. After chiseling about 5 in (12.7 cm) through the masonry, they broke into the Southern Airshaft. They noticed it was about 8 in (20.3 cm) square. It went vertically for about 6 ft (2 m) and then disappeared upward out of sight. They also found the airshaft in the northern wall by chiseling through this wall in the same location. They tried to locate the exit points of these shafts but could not find any. They even lit a fire in the shafts and did not observe the smoke escaping to the outside. Why were these shafts sealed off with 5 in (12.7 cm) of masonry at their ends? Where did they lead?

SUBTERRANEAN CHAMBERS

The Descending Passage has the same dimensions as the Ascending Passage; it is 3 ft 6 in (1 m) wide by almost 4 ft (1.2 m) high. It slopes down at an angle of 26 degrees. The distance of the Descending Passage to the beginning of the horizontal Subterranean Chamber Passage is about 344 ft (74 m). This shorter horizontal section leads to the Lesser Subterranean Chamber and then continues into the large Subterranean Chamber.

This large chamber is a strange place. It is about 11 ft (3.3 m) high with a floor area of 46 ft by 27 ft (14 m by 8 m). It is cut deep into the bedrock almost 600 ft (183 m) directly below the apex of the pyramid. Its ceiling is smooth and the floor is cut in several rough levels, making it look unfinished. It has also been referred to as the "upside down room." When the Arabs first broke into the pyramid in 820 CE, they found torch

The Bottomless Pit

In the center of the Subterranean Chamber on the east side is a square pit, known as the "Bottomless Pit." It is so called because at the time of its discovery, it was not known how deep it was. In 1838 the pit was measured to be 12 ft (4 m) deep. However, Colonel Vyse, who was searching for hidden chambers, had it dug deeper.

marks on the ceiling showing that someone had entered the pyramid before them and had explored these lower chambers.

In 1909, John and Edgar Morton, two brothers from Scotland, visited the pyramid. Their account states that: "In the unfinished floor of the Subterranean Chamber appears the large, squarish mouth of a deep vertical shaft. We had always to avoid walking too near its edge, for the rough uneven floor of the chamber is covered with loose crumbling debris."

In the south wall, opposite the entrance, is a low, narrow passage which runs 53 ft (16.1 m) before coming to a blind end. When the Morton brothers explored this passage, they found that the floor was covered with dark earthy mould, 2 to 3 in (5 to 7 cm) deep.

THE WELL SHAFT

At the intersection where the Ascending Passage meets with the Grand Gallery is a hole leading to a shaft (known as the Well Shaft), which connects with the Descending Passage below. It was discovered in 1637 by the Oxford astronomer John Greaves. This near-vertical tunnel is about 3 ft (1 m) in diameter. As it continues downward for 60 ft (18 m), a grotto opens off the shaft. It is thought that the grotto may have been a natural hole that was enlarged during the building of the Well Shaft. Inside the grotto, there is a large block of cut stone, the purpose of which is unknown. The shaft then continues downward to connect with the lower part of the Descending Passage. The purpose of the Well Shaft remains a mystery.

Greaves published his investigations in 1646 under the title *Pyramidographia: A Description of the Pyramids in Egypt*. This was the first scientific study ever published on the Great Pyramid. His work provided a great stimulus to other investigators, and English, French, German, Dutch, and Italian explorers soon followed him.

LEFT
The north-west corner of the Subterranean Chamber. This photograph was taken by John and Morton Edgar in 1909.

Inside the Queen's Chamber

Colonel Vyse also dug up the floor in the Queen's Chamber but, after finding only an old basket, he refilled the holes. Whatever happened to this basket is a mystery. The Niche in the Queen's Chamber was originally about 3 ½ ft (1 m) deep, but explorers have hacked deeper into it and it is currently several yards deep.

BELOW
The Subterranean Chamber, showing the east wall and ceiling. This large chamber has a floor area of 46 ft by 27 ft (14 m by 8 m) and an average height of 11 ft (3.3 m). It is almost 600 ft (183 m) below the apex of the pyramid, cut deep into the bedrock.

CHAPTER FIVE

THE SEARCH FOR SECRETS

The search for hidden chambers in ancient structures is a fascinating aspect of archeology. Since the 1960s, scientific equipment has been employed in an attempt to detect secret passageways and lost artifacts within the Great Pyramid.

The possibility of discovering hidden chambers or passages in the Great Pyramid has interested scholars and lay people alike for thousands of years. The idea of finding hidden treasures, the blueprints of the pyramid, lost scientific information, and technological devices of a lost culture has motivated people to search for hidden chambers within this pyramid as well as in other ancient structures. Before the 20th century, the only way of conducting this type of exploration was to bore into the structure, hoping by luck to hit an undiscovered passage or chamber. Now we have modern scientific instruments to help us continue the search.

In the past, experiments have been conducted using sophisticated equipment, which records measurements of magnetic fields, sound waves, and other energy fields, to try to discover hidden chambers within these structures. Cosmic ray probes, developed by Dr. Louis Alvarez (who won the Nobel Prize in physics), were used in 1968 by Alvarez and Dr. Ahmed Fahkry, an Egyptologist, to try to find hidden chambers in Chephren's Pyramid (the second largest pyramid).

COSMIC RAYS

Cosmic rays continually bombard our planet. They lose some of their energy as they penetrate rocks. If there are hollow spaces in the rock, the rays lose less energy than if the rock was solid. A spark chamber can measure the energy of these rays and record the information on tape. A spark chamber was placed in a chamber (46 ft by 20 ft by 16 ft/14 m by 6 m by 5 m) at the base of Chephren's Pyramid. It appeared that something strange was going on. The oscilloscopes (electronic devices that trace voltage and current) showed a chaotic pattern, and each time the data was run through the computer different results came out. No one was able to discover why this was happening. The results were inconclusive and no hidden chambers were found.

HIDDEN CHAMBERS

In 1974, a team from Stanford University, California, and the Ains Shams University, Cairo, attempted to find hidden chambers using an electromagnetic sounder. Unfortunately, because of certain environmental problems (including moisture in the Great Pyramid), this method was not conclusive and was abandoned.

ABOVE

The Lesser Subterranean Chamber and Subterranean Chamber Passage.

PREVIOUS PAGE

The possibility of discovering hidden treasure or ancient knowledge within the Great Pyramid has motivated many people to search for hidden chambers within it.

Later, in 1986, two French architects used electronic detectors to try to locate hollow areas. They found that below the passageway leading to the Queen's Chamber was another chamber (9 ft by 15 ft/3 m by 5 m). They bored a 1-in (2.5-cm) hole and found a cavity filled with crystalline silica (sand). Further digging was prohibited by the authorities, and no entrances to these areas have yet been found.

This sand was analyzed and found to contain more than 99 percent quartz, which varied between 100 and 400 microns in size. This kind of sand is known as musical sand because it makes a whispering noise when it is blown or walked on.

It appears that this sand may come from El Tur in southern Sinai, which is several hundred miles from the Great Pyramid. This creates another mystery. Why would this type of sand have been brought from so far away and placed in a sealed-off chamber in the Great Pyramid?

X-RAYS & RADAR

In 1987, Japanese researchers from Waseda University used X-rays to look for hollow spaces and chambers. They claimed to have discovered a labyrinth of corridors and chambers inside the Great Pyramid. They found a cavity about 4 ¾ ft (1.5 m) under the horizontal passage to the

Queen's Chamber and extending for almost 9 ft (3 m). They also identified a cavity behind the western part of the northern wall of the Queen's Chamber. Other investigators have been unable to confirm this, but it is hoped that more scientific studies will verify these results.

In 1988 another Japanese team identified a cavity off the Horizontal Passage, near to where the French team drilled in 1986. A large cavity was also detected behind the north-west wall of the Queen's Chamber. Further investigations were prevented by the Egyptian government.

In 1992, ground-penetrating radar and micro-gravimetric measurements were made in the Bottomless Pit (see page 38) in the Subterranean Chamber, and in the Subterranean Chamber Passage connecting the bottom of the Descending Passage with the Subterranean Chamber. A structure was detected under the floor of the passage. Another structure was detected on the western side of the passageway about 16 ft (5 m) from the entrance to the Subterranean Chamber. Soundings studies indicate that it is a vertical shaft about 4 ft 7 in (1.4 m) square and 16 ft (5 m) deep.

It is interesting to speculate about these chambers. What was their purpose and do they still contain anything that could help us solve some of the unanswered questions about the Great Pyramid? We wait to see if further studies are permitted in the near future.

ABOVE
The north-east corner of the Subterranean Chamber, showing the square doorway of the small horizontal passage.

LEFT
Cross section of the Queen's Chamber, showing the Niche. The Niche is just over 16 ft (5 m) high, and some believe it once contained a statue, although no evidence for this has been found.

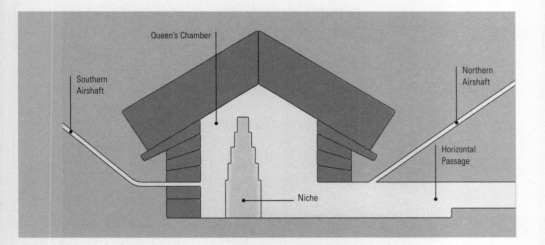

LEFT
Cross section of the Subterranean Chamber, showing the Descending Passage and the Well Shaft.

FAR LEFT
Evidence suggests that sand found in a hidden chamber leading to the Queen's Chamber is from El Tur in southern Sinai, several hundred miles from the Great Pyramid.

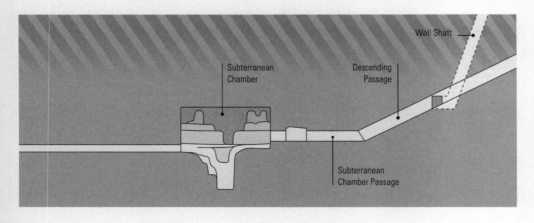

BELOW

Upuaut, the miniature robot with a camera used by Rudolf Gantenbrink in 1993 to explore the shafts of the Queen's Chamber.

EXPLORING THE QUEEN'S CHAMBER AIRSHAFTS

One of the most exciting aspects of exploring the Great Pyramid is looking for hidden chambers. After the discovery of airshafts in the Queen's Chamber in 1872, many attempts have been made to explore them. In 1993 a robot named Upuaut was employed for this purpose.

The discovery of the Queen's Chamber airshafts (see page 38) raised more questions. Where did they lead to and what was their purpose? It had been known since the 1800s that the airshafts from the King's Chamber exited to the outside of the pyramid and the actual exit points have been located. As no exit points have been found from the Queen's Chamber airshafts it has been assumed that they end inside the pyramid—possibly in a secret or hidden chamber.

THE SOUTHERN AIRSHAFT

In the last few decades, technological advances have allowed both of the shafts, which are about 8 in² (20.3 cm²), to be explored. In 1993, a German engineer, Rudolf Gantenbrink, used Upuaut, a miniature robot fitted with a camera, to explore the Southern Airshaft leading out of the chamber. This robot was a very sophisticated device; its manufacture cost was about a quarter of a million dollars. It fitted into the opening of the airshaft and was controlled by an attached cable.

Gantenbrink and his staff positioned the robot deep within the small airshaft at the southern end of the Queen's Chamber and moved it very slowly upward. The camera monitored the robot's progress as it moved up the airshaft. As it proceeded, it sent back some of the first images of the inside of the airshaft. The robot finally came to the end of its journey after traveling about 200 ft (61 m) upward within the airshaft. It revealed that the airshaft did not lead to the outside, but directly in front of the robot was a small door with two copper handles. It appeared that there was a little gap under the door. There was not enough room for the robot to go under nor for the camera to see under the door. Thus, there was another mystery to investigate. What was behind the door?

Gantenbrink had plans to pursue the exploration of the airshaft, but unfortunately the Egyptian authorities did not allow him to continue. The robot is currently in the British Museum, and nothing further came of this exploration until many years later.

FURTHER ROBOT EXPLORATION

In 1995, Zahi Hawass, Director of the Giza Plateau, announced that there would be a further exploration of the door leading to the alleged

BELOW

In 2002 an exploration with a new robot was approved. The robot was fitted with a camera and a high powered drill, and was sent up the Southern Airshaft.

hidden chamber sometime in 1996. This never happened. Dr. Hawass stated again in 1998 that he hoped to explore the shaft. Again, nothing happened. It was also rumored that the door at the end of the airshaft would be opened during the Egyptian millennium celebrations at the Giza Plateau. This also never happened.

The big day finally came on September 16, 2002, when millions of people all over the world watched the exploration on television. An exploration with a new robot had been approved by the Egyptian authorities and the robot was sent up the Southern Airshaft. Designed by iRobot of Boston, U.S.A., it was mounted with a camera, a measuring device, and a high-powered drill. A measuring apparatus was used to try to determine how thick the door was and whether a drill could penetrate it, thus allowing the camera to look inside. It found that the door was only 3 in (7.6 cm) thick, suggesting that it might lead to another chamber. The robot drilled a small hole in the wall. When the camera looked through, it appeared that there was a small empty chamber and another stone door blocking the way. This next door appeared to be sealed, and the Egyptian authorities decided not to drill through it. The millions viewing this event were disappointed that the exploration ended in this way.

Unknown to the general public, several days later, a robot was sent up to explore the Northern Airshaft. It too discovered a door that blocked this shaft. The doors in both shafts are 208 ft (63.3 m) from the Queen's Chamber. It would appear that the Northern Airshaft extended to the north as far as the Southern Airshaft extended to the south. The northern shaft door appeared to be similar to the door in the southern shaft, and it also has a pair of copper handles.

No further exploration has been undertaken since, although in 2006 it was rumored that two different international teams were competing to send a robot up the shaft. Nothing has been reported since, so we still wait and hope.

ABOVE
The door with metal handles found by Upuaut at the end of the Southern Airshaft of the Queen's Chamber. There is a very small gap under the door.

BELOW
It was rumored that the door at the end of the airshaft would be opened during the millennium celebrations.

ANCIENT ARTIFACTS

Before the 1800s, extensive searches of the Great Pyramid over the centuries did not yield any treasure—neither gold artifacts, nor jewels, nor written works. However, more recently several items of great archeological interest have been found.

In 1836 Colonel Vyse discovered and removed a flat iron plate with a surface area of about 12 in by 4 in (30 cm by 10 cm) and ⅛ inch (0.0635 cm) thick from a joint in the masonry at the point where the Southern Airshaft from the King's Chamber exits the pyramid. Engineers agree that this plate was left in the joint during the building of the pyramid and could not have been inserted afterwards. Colonel Vyse sent the plate to the British Museum. The famous archeologist Sir Flinders Petrie examined the plate in 1881. He judged it to be authentic and stated that, "no reasonable doubt can therefore exist about its being a really genuine piece." Then, in 1989, it was analyzed both by Dr. M.P. Jones in the Department of Mineral Resources Engineering at Imperial College, London, and by Dr. Sayed El Gayer in the Department of Petroleum and Mining Engineering at the Suez Canal University, Egypt. They used both chemical and optical tests.

One hypothesis was that the metal might have come from a meteorite. It has been well documented that primitive and Stone Age peoples often used meteorite iron for implements, such as tools and ritual objects. They were able to make crude iron implements from the meteorite iron well before the Iron Age. In fact, wrapped in King Tutankhamun's mummy was a dagger made of meteorite iron. Whether such metal is from a meteorite or from the Earth can be determined by the nickel content of the

iron. Meteorite iron has a higher value than the iron found on Earth. The analysis of the metal plate showed that it was not of meteoritic origin, since it contains only a trace of nickel and is not at the higher level of meteoritic iron.

Further analysis revealed that it had traces of gold on its surface, indicating that it may once have been gold-plated. In their written analysis, Drs. Jones and Gayer concluded that the iron plate was ancient and that the evidence suggested the plate was incorporated within the pyramid at the time that the structure was built. They also thought this plate might have been a fragment from a larger piece, which was fitted over the mouth of the airshaft. So far, a larger piece has not been found.

The discovery of the iron plate has had momentous consequences. Given that the Great Pyramid was probably constructed around 2550 BCE, this may mean that the generally accepted date of the beginning of the Iron Age (around 1200 BCE) is out by more than 2,000 years.

AIRSHAFT HAUL

Waynman Dixon, the engineer who discovered the openings of the Queen's Chamber airshafts in 1872 (see page 38), also discovered some very interesting objects in the Northern Airshaft of the Queen's Chamber.

A little way up the airshaft, he found three objects: a rough stone sphere, a small two-pronged hook made of some kind of indiscernible metal, and a 4 in (12 cm) long piece of cedarwood with notches cut into it. Dixon brought these objects to Britain when he returned. Within a short period of

time they had disappeared. Recently, it was found that they had remained in the hands of the Dixon family and were donated to the British Museum in the 1970s. No one knows what happened to these objects at the British Museum, but it appears that they were just stored away and forgotten about. They reappeared again in 1990. It is interesting to note that the cedarwood artifact was missing. If this wood could be carbon dated, perhaps it would reveal the year of the building of the Great Pyramid.

As mentioned on page 44, in 1993 Rudolf Gantenbrink explored the Southern Airshaft with his robot. He also sent the robot up the Northern Airshaft for a short distance beyond where Dixon had found his artifacts. The find was recorded on video. The robot discovered two artifacts: a metallic hook and a long piece of wood. If it were possible to remove this wood, it could be carbon dated and provide more clues about the pyramid.

BEYOND THE AIRSHAFT DOORS

What lies behind the second door in the Southern Airshaft and the first door in the Northern Airshaft remains a mystery for now. To remove and examine some of the artifacts remaining in the Northern Airshaft, and even a sample of the copper handles on the doors in the Southern Airshaft, would be a boon. It appears from the photographs that some of the copper has broken off and is on the ground by the door. If this could be retrieved, it may be possible to have it analyzed.

Many scientists are trying to develop other means of discovering hidden chambers and passages in the Great Pyramid and in other Egyptian monuments and structures. It is hoped that one day a hidden chamber will be found that will reveal information about our past of which we were previously unaware. For the time being, however, we have to wait to see what is behind those sealed doors.

ABOVE
The tomb of Tutankhamun. A dagger made of meteorite iron was found wrapped in Tutankhamun's mummy.

BELOW
The northern shaft of the Queen's Chamber, showing the long piece of wood on the floor. If this could be removed, carbon dating could be done.

CHAPTER SIX

MEMORIES AND MYTHS

In this chapter we will explore some of the many ancient legends about the Great Pyramid. It is very interesting to read what ancient writers had to say about the purpose of the Great Pyramid, since so many of the current theories are, in fact, variations of these legends.

I t is not surprising that there are so many myths and legends about the purpose of the Great Pyramid. Even though it would be impossible to discern which are true and which are false, they are fascinating in their own right. Often we find that the legends are hung on a real historical event. And, if we study the myths closely enough, a common denominator may emerge, which could show the way to the truth.

It is interesting that no description of the Great Pyramid has survived from any known Egyptian text or description. It is possible that some day we may find a papyrus or inscription somewhere, but for the moment we must rely on the earliest writings and legends.

GREEK HISTORIES

The first known eyewitness, Thales, the father of Greek geometry in the sixth century BCE, supposedly calculated the height of the Great Pyramid by measuring its shadow at the same time of day as when the length of his own shadow was equal to his height.

The earliest written record of the Great Pyramid comes from the Greek historian Herodotus, who lived in the fifth century BCE and visited the pyramids in 440 BCE. Known as the "Father of History," Herodotus traveled widely and visited Egypt, where he conversed with priests who told him about Egypt's history. He recorded what he had learned in his book, *Histories*. At the time Herodotus visited the pyramids, they were still covered in their limestone casing stones. Other ancient classical writers who mentioned the Great Pyramid include Euhemerus, a Greek writer who lived in the fourth century BCE, Eratosthenes, in the third century BCE, and Dionysius of Halicarnassus, in the first century BCE. These early witnesses are important since they could provide clues about the Great Pyramid before much of its destruction by erosion, earthquakes, explorers, etcetera.

Although most historians do not accept Herodotus' writings as a valid historical account, he does provide a fascinating story about the construction of the Great Pyramid and the surrounding complex. In his book "*Histories*," he writes:

"One hundred thousand men worked at a time and were relieved every three months by a fresh party. It took ten years' arduous toil by the people to make the causeway for the conveyance of the stones, a work, in my opinion, not much inferior to the pyramid itself, for its length is five stadia and its width ten orgyae and its height where it is highest, eight orgyae; it is built of polished stone with carvings of animals on it. The pyramid itself took thirty years to build. It is square, each side is eight plethra and the height is the same: it is composed of polished stones and jointed with the greatest exactness; none of the stones are less than 30 ft (9 m). This pyramid was built thus: in the form of steps which some call crossae, others bomides. When they had laid the first stones in this manner, they raised the remaining stones by machines made of short planks of wood: having lifted them from the ground to the first range of steps, when the stone arrived there, it was put on another machine that stood ready on the first range; and from this it was drawn to the second range on another machine; for the machines were equal in

Conflicting Accounts

Herodotus writes that Khufu (the supposed builder of the Great Pyramid) was a bad king since he shut down all the temples in Egypt and oppressed his people. Manetho, an Egyptian high priest and historian from the third century BCE was more favorable and said that King Khufu, "built the largest Pyramid … was translated to the Gods and wrote the Sacred Book."

Pyramid Inscription

Herodotus also writes that:
"On the pyramid there is an inscription
in Egyptian characters which records the
amount expended on radishes, onions, and
garlic for the workmen: which the interpreter,
as I well remember, reading the inscription,
told me amounted to one thousand six
hundred talents of silver. And if this be really
true, how much more must have been spent
on iron tools, on bread, and on clothes for the
workmen, since they occupied in building
the work the time which I mentioned and in
addition, no short time, I imagine, in cutting
and drawing the stones and in forming the
underground excavation."

number to the ranges of steps; or they removed the
machine, which was only one, and portable, to each
range in succession, whenever they wished to raise
the stone higher; for I should relate it in both ways,
as it is related. The upper portion of the pyramid
was finished first; then the middle and finally the
part that is lowest and nearest to the ground."

MORE CLASSICAL ACCOUNTS

Other classical writers such as Diodorus Siculus,
Strabo, and Pliny the Elder mention the Great
Pyramid in passing. Diodorus Siculus, who lived in
the first century BCE, was born in Sicily and wrote
the history of the world in forty books. He described
the pyramid's casing stones at that time as being,
"complete and without the least decay." He wrote:

"Although these kings [Khufu and Chephren]
intended these [pyramids] for their sepulchers, yet
it happened that neither of them was buried there.
The largest [pyramid] is quadrangular; each side

LEFT
Sculpture of Chephren, the
son of Khufu. Although it
is widely believed that the
pyramids were built to bury
Chephren and Khufu, there is
no evidence to support this.

RIGHT

Illustration of the entrance to the Great Pyramid by George Sandys, 1610. The Greek geographer Strabo wrote that the entrance to the Great Pyramid was lost during the first centuries CE.

BELOW

Wall painting from the tomb of Sennedjem, showing the moon (or possibly a solar disc) and seven stars. The Arab historian Masoudi wrote that the Great Pyramid was inscribed with figures representing the stars and planets, as well as with the position of the stars and their cycles.

at its base is 7 plethra and more than 6 plethra high; it gradually contracts to the top where each side is 6 cubits; it is built entirely of solid stone, of a different workmanship, but eternal duration; for in the thousands of years said to have elapsed since their construction ... the stones have not moved from their original position, but the whole remains uninjured. The stone is said to have been brought from a great distance in Arabia and raised on mounds, for machines, in those days, had not been invented."

Strabo, the Greek geographer, visited the Great Pyramid in 24 CE. He wrote seventeen books called *Geographia*, and this is what he had to say regarding the entrance to the Great Pyramid:

"A little way up one side, is a stone that may be taken out, which being raised up, there is a sloping passage to the foundations."

As noted earlier, the location of this entrance on the north side of the pyramid consisted of a hinged stone that could be raised to enter the pyramid and that was indistinguishable from the surrounding limestone blocks when closed. It was lost during the first centuries CE.

Josephus, the Hebrew historian of the first century CE, gives a very interesting account in his book, *Antiquities*. Josephus states that, "the descendants of Seth [the third son of Adam and Eve], after perfecting their study of astronomy, set out for Egypt, and there embodied their discoveries in the building of:

"Two pillars [i.e. monuments], one in stone and the other in brick, in order that this knowledge might not be lost before these discoveries were sufficiently known, upon Adam's prediction that the world was to be destroyed by a flood ... and in order to exhibit them to mankind ... Now this pillar remains in the land of Siriad [the Siriadic, or Dogstar, land of Egypt] to this day." Could this pillar in Egypt be the Great Pyramid of Giza?

There is a similar tradition ascribed to Enoch, the Hebrew Patriarch mentioned in the Bible:

"Enoch, foreseeing the destruction of the earth, inscribed the science of astronomy upon two pillars."

ARAB ACCOUNTS

In 850 CE, the first written version of the Arabian Nights was translated into Arabic—thirty years after the Great Pyramid was finally penetrated by Arab excavators (820 CE). This was a book of Persian tales called *Hazar Afsanah* (*A Thousand Legends*). In these tales, the Great Pyramid was imputed to have magical powers and contain magnificent treasures.

The Arab historian, Masoudi (who died in 967 CE) cites a similar legend. He writes that the three pyramids of Giza were built as a result of a dream that appeared to King Surid (see pages 54–55), in which the Flood was foretold 300 years before it actually occurred:

"It is told that he ordered the priests to deposit within the pyramids written accounts of their wisdom and acquirements in the different arts and sciences ... and of arithmetic and geometry that they might remain as records for the benefit of those who would afterwards be able to comprehend them."

One of the earliest legends was passed down from an Arab writer, Ben Mohammed Balki, who stated that the three Giza pyramids were built as a refuge against the destruction of mankind either by fire or by water.

The Arab writer, Ibn Abd-al-Latif, who lived in the 12th century CE, said that the second pyramid was:

"Filled with a store of riches and utensils ... with arms which rust not, and with glass which might be bended and yet not broken."

Masoudi also stated that:

"The Great Pyramid was inscribed with the heavenly spheres, and figures representing the stars and planets in the forms in which they were worshipped. Also the position of the stars and their cycles ... the history and chronicles of time past, of that which is to come, and of every future event which would take place in Egypt."

Another source echoes the belief that ancient wisdom was enshrined in the Great Pyramid. It states that written upon the walls of the pyramid

were, "the mysteries of science, astronomy, physics, and such useful knowledge which any person understanding our writing can read."

WHERE IS THE EVIDENCE?

Is there any evidence to confirm that the Great Pyramid was once covered with these writings? Since the original casing stones were destroyed and removed for the building of mosques after an earthquake in 1301 CE, we do not know if there was any original writing upon them. It does not seem likely because there still remain some casing stones at the pyramid's lowest level, and they do not have any inscriptions on them.

ABOVE
An engraving of a sphere model of the Heavens. Masoudi also wrote that the Great Pyramid was inscribed with the heavenly spheres, as well as with the history of time past, and all future events to take place in Egypt.

LEFT
A mosaic in the Basilica of San Marco, Venice, showing Noah releasing a dove from the Ark. Some ancient accounts of the Great Pyramid claim that it was built to enshrine knowledge before the Earth was destroyed by a flood, or as a refuge from destruction by fire or water.

A KING'S DREAM

Many of the myths and legends about the Great Pyramid are fanciful, but they demonstrate how it has occupied the minds and imagination of people throughout the Ages. Many of these legends are attributed to the Arabs. Below is an interesting story about the Great Pyramid, as told by Murtadi, son of Gaphiphus, in 992 CE at Tithe, Arabia. This extract is taken from The Egyptian History:

"There was a king named Saurid, the son of Sahaloe, 300 years before the Deluge, who dreamed one night that he saw the earth overturned with its inhabitants, the men cast down on their faces, the stars falling out of the heavens, and striking one against the other, and making horrid and dreadful cries as they fell. He thereupon awoke much troubled. A year after he dreamed again that he saw the fixed stars come down to the earth in the form of white birds, which carried men away, and cast them between two great mountains, which almost joined together and covered them; and then the bright, shining stars became dark and were eclipsed. Next morning he ordered all the princes of the priests, and magicians of all the provinces of Egypt, to meet together; which they did to the

number of 130 priests and soothsayers, with whom he went and related to them his dream.

"Among others, the priest Aclimon, who was the greatest of all, and resided chiefly in the King's Court, said thus to him: 'I myself had a dream about a year ago which frightened me very much, and which I have not revealed to anyone. I dreamed,' said the priest, 'that I was with your Majesty on the top of the mountain of fire, which is in the midst of Emosos, and that I saw the heaven sink down below its ordinary situation, so that it was near the crown of our heads, covering and surrounding us, like a great basin turned upside down; that the stars were intermingled among men in diverse figures; that the people implored your Majesty's succor, and ran to you in multitudes as their refuge; that you lifted up your hands above your head, and endeavored to thrust back the heaven, and keep it from coming down so low; and that I, seeing what your Majesty did, did also the same. While we were in that posture, extremely affrighted, I thought we saw a certain part of heaven opening, and a bright light coming out of it; that afterwards the sun rose out of the same place, and we began to implore his assistance;

whereupon he said thus to us: "The heaven will return to its ordinary situation when I shall have performed three hundred courses." I thereupon awaked extremely affrighted.'

"The priest having thus spoken, the king commanded them to take the height of the stars, and to consider what accident they portended. Whereupon they declared that they promised first the Deluge, and after that fire. Then he commanded pyramids should be built, that they might remove and secure in them what was of most esteem in their treasuries, with the bodies of the kings, and their wealth, and the aromatic roots which served them, and that they should write their wisdom upon them, that the violence of the water might not destroy it."

Inscribed Knowledge

Another early Arab historian adds to the story: "And he [Saurid] filled them [the pyramids] with talismans, and with strange things, and with riches and treasures and the like. He engraved in them all things that were told him by wise men, as, also, all profound sciences. The names of alakakirs, the uses and hurts of them, the science of astrology and of arithmetic, of geometry and physics. All these may be interpreted by him who knows their characters and language ..."

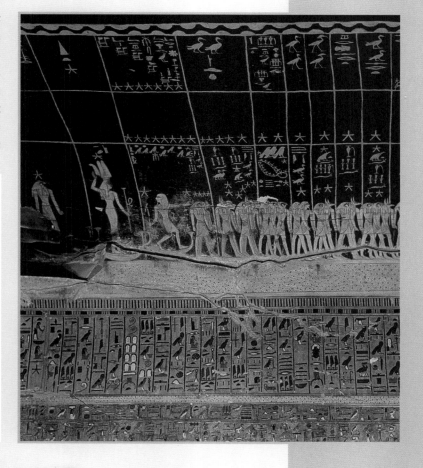

PART TWO

THE THEORIES

"There is still no definite answer to the question: Who built the Great Pyramid of Giza and when?"

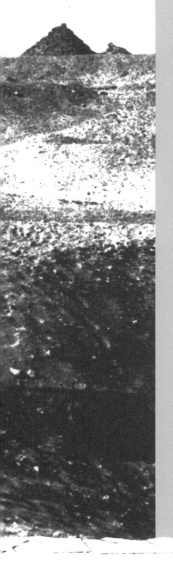

CHAPTER SEVEN

WHO, WHEN, AND HOW?

It may seem strange, but there is still no definitive answer to the question: Who built the Great Pyramid of Giza and when? There are, however, many fascinating theories. Most academic Egyptologists accept that the Great Pyramid was built during the reign of the Pharaoh Khufu during the Fourth Dynasty, around 2550 BCE. What evidence is there to support this theory?

The only real evidence has been the discovery of red ocher markings in some of the relieving chambers above the King's Chamber. These markings have been in question ever since the famous explorer Colonel Howard Vyse first discovered them in the 19th century. He explored the Great Pyramid in 1836 and found the additional four relieving chambers above Davison's Chamber.

Vyse claimed to have discovered inscriptions in a red pigment painted on the walls of these chambers. He identified them as quarry marks, inscribed so that the stones used in building the Great Pyramid would reach their destination and the workers would know where to place them. As we have seen, Vyse also claimed to have discovered cartouches (the names of Pharaohs), and one of them bore the name "Khufu." If authentic, they could date the Great Pyramid to the time of Khufu.

It is interesting to note that no other quarry marks were found elsewhere in the pyramid, and these appear to be the only inscriptions ever found in the Great Pyramid.

KHUFU'S CARTOUCHE

But on close examination of the Khufu cartouche, it appears that these hieroglyphics were a type not used until hundreds of years later in Egypt. Some have also claimed that there is a misspelling in Khufu's name. Coincidentally, the same misspelling appeared in a hieroglyphic textbook at that time, to which Colonel Vyse would have had access. So we have an inscription that is at least 200 years ahead of its time and has a misspelling that was found in a hieroglyphic textbook contemporaneous with Vyse. This evidence leads many to conclude that he forged those marks to make a name for himself.

THE DATING OF THE GIZA COMPLEX

Egyptologist and author John Anthony West and geologist Dr. Robert Schoch of Boston University have recently challenged academic Egyptologists' dating of the Sphinx. They have also put forward that the weathering on the body of the Sphinx and the Sphinx enclosure has not been eroded by wind-blown sand but, in fact, by water.

ABOVE
Sphinxes are considered to be mythical creatures and guardians. The Sphinx on the Giza Plateau faces due east, toward the rising sun. Some believe it is the head of the Pharaoh Chephren, but there is no conclusive proof of this. Most researchers believe it is much older than the time of the fourth Egyptian dynasty.

PREVIOUS PAGE
The Sphinx with the Great Pyramid in the background.

Other geologists that Dr. Schoch consulted on the matter have agreed with him. So when were the last major rainfalls in Egypt that could account for this erosion of the Sphinx? Paleo-climatological studies show that heavy rains in Egypt had stopped by 10000 BCE. Egypt then became a desert and has been ever since. So, if the erosion of the Sphinx was caused by rainfall, it would date it to this time and thus make it at least 7,000 years older than previously thought. This water erosion pattern was also seen on the Sphinx wall enclosure and other nearby structures. Thus, this may be one way of dating the Giza complex.

This is a very hotly debated area among researchers, and the truth is that more geological studies need to be done, and additional dating methods used, to try to determine the true date of the Giza complex.

CARBON DATING

In 1986, a study was conducted on the Great Pyramid in which sixty-four mortar samples were removed and carbon dated. Two samples were tested at the Southern Methodist University in Dallas, and thirteen samples were tested in Zurich. This carbon dating indicated a range of 3809 BCE to 2869 BCE. This figure is about 500 years older than academic Egyptologists have accepted as the building date of the Great Pyramid. Experts have questioned the validity of this test for several reasons. Carbon dating is not always reliable and certain archeological samples do not lend themselves to this technique. Also, the mortar could be from later repairs to the pyramid. Thus, the validity of carbon dating is questionable here and further studies need to be done.

LOST CIVILIZATION

Geological evidence indicates that the Great Pyramid is thousands of years older than previously thought. If the ancient Egyptians did not build it, then who did? Some authors have speculated that people from the legendary city of Atlantis built it with the incredible technology some believe they had at their disposal. Others have speculated that aliens may have visited the Earth long ago and constructed the Great Pyramid using alien technology. Other possibilities that have been suggested include biblical figures such as Seth, Enoch, Shem, Noah, or Melchizedek. Without concrete data, all we can do is speculate.

The carbon dating and lack of solid evidence linking Khufu to the Great Pyramid lead many to conclude that the dynastic Egyptians did not build it. It is also apparent that they did not possess the technology to construct this magnificent structure. Unfortunately, at this stage we do not have a clear idea who built the Great Pyramid. Until we obtain concrete proof, the question of who and when remains a mystery.

LEFT

A painting from 1883 by Ernst Koerner showing the excavation of the Sphinx. There is much debate about just how old the Sphinx actually is.

BELOW

A map showing one of the possible locations of the legendary island of Atlantis.

Dating the Great Pyramid

Can we scientifically date the building of the Great Pyramid? One of the first individuals to question the dating of structures on the Giza Plateau was Symbolist and Egyptologist, R.A. Schwaller de Lubicz (1887–1961). He observed that the Sphinx had not been eroded by sand, as most academic Egyptologists believe, but by water, i.e. rainfall.

HOW WAS IT BUILT?

Even though there have been numerous theories proposed as to how the Great Pyramid was built, none are definitive. We must keep in mind that the ancient Egyptians did not have knowledge of the wheel and pulley, although they did make use of levers, rollers, and ropes. Many theories assume that these devices were used to build the Great Pyramid.

LEFT
Illustration of Jewish slaves building the pyramids using ropes and rollers.

ABOVE
AND RIGHT
Primitive tools such as copper chisels and wooden mallets were all that the Egyptians had at their disposal.

One major theory as to how the Great Pyramid of Giza was built proposes the use of encircling ramps. The ramps would continually wrap around the pyramid as it was built, and stones were hauled up them using sledges and rollers. Other theories propose one very long ramp that stretched out into the desert. As the pyramid grew in height, this ramp was also raised higher and lengthened as needed. Blocks were hauled up the ramp using sledges and ropes.

If we consider the size and weight of the blocks (the average is about 2 ½ tons/2,268 kg), the number of blocks, and the size of the completed pyramid itself, it is apparent that neither of these theories can explain how it was built. The ramp method has been tested, and to build even a very small pyramid using these proposed mechanical devices that were supposedly available to the Egyptians has proved extremely difficult.

If we were to assume that the Great Pyramid was built using these methods around 2550 BCE during the reign of Khufu (his reign lasted a little over twenty years), we would also have to assume that all his workers toiled twenty-four hours a day, every day, and that they dressed and laid every block at the rate of one every ninety seconds. This is an impossible feat, bearing in mind the primitive tools that the Egyptians had at

LEFT
Fragment of a tomb relief
showing carpenters working
with primitive tools.

BELOW
A stonemason performs
modern restoration work in
Giza using the same tools that
would have been available to
the ancient Egyptians.

their disposal. Also, it would have been impossible for them to construct the interior passageways and magnificent chambers with such incredible precision and orientation, using only the copper chisels, adzes, and wooden mallets that were available to them.

Not only does it seem impossible that the Egyptians built the Great Pyramid with these primitive hand tools but, as we have seen, current research suggests that the Great Pyramid is considerably older than academic researchers had previously thought. This leads to speculation as to whether the pyramid could have been built using advanced scientific knowledge.

ABOVE

An inscribed papyrus. One
historical account from the
tenth century claims that
the ancient Egyptians placed
leaves of inscribed papyrus
under heavy blocks of stone
to levitate them.

THE LEVITATION THEORY

Did the builders of the Great Pyramid, whoever they were, have advanced scientific knowledge unknown to us? Is this how the Great Pyramid and other grand structures that defy "conventional" explanation were built? One theory is that some form of levitation was used to lift the heavy limestone and granite blocks. Is there any evidence that this method was used, either from historical records or scientific experiments?

Let us first look at some historical records. Masoudi, an Arab historian of the tenth century, wrote that the Egyptians used magic spells to move large blocks: "In carrying on the work, leaves of papyrus, or paper, inscribed with certain characters, were placed under the stones prepared in the quarries; and upon being struck, the blocks were moved at each time the distance of a bowshot [which would be a little over 200 ft/60 m], and so by degrees arrived at the pyramids."

Did Masoudi make up this story, or is there some truth in it? Was he reporting on an early legend that the blocks were moved mysteriously, and he added the story of the inscribed papyrus to embellish? Or were the blocks placed on some unknown apparatus (mistaken by the historian for a papyrus leaf) that would levitate them? If you strip away all the additions and embellishments to a legend, sometimes you are left with a grain of truth.

In modern times, there have been many reports by travelers to the East (India, Tibet, China, etcetera) that holy men or ascetics have the ability to levitate objects. Again, could this effect be produced by sleight of hand, imagination, or suggestion? It appears that there are too many of these stories by reliable witnesses to dismiss the possibility that these holy men developed some sort of ability to levitate objects. More recently, followers of Maharishi Mahesh Yogi (founder of Transcendental Meditation) have claimed through a specific program of training and discipline to be able to levitate.

Could levitation have been used to lift the heavy blocks from which the Great Pyramid was built? With scientific developments in areas such as quantum mechanics and string theory, our old theories are constantly being challenged and revised. I have always believed that this new area of physics is very similar to some of the metaphysical ideas of current times. Is it possible that science and metaphysics will meet and help to explain how phenomena that currently seem to be supernatural are actually higher laws of physics? Perhaps the ancients had knowledge that we are just beginning to discover.

Magical Construction

There are many other legends of the construction of temples and buildings using mysterious or magical means to lift blocks. These stories abound in Mayan and Greek legends, and also in the Bible. In the opposite sense, marching around the walls, the blowing of trumpets, and shouting brought down the walls of Jericho. Maybe we could call this "anti-levitation."

SOUND LEVITATION

Throughout history, levitation has been associated with magic, but recently levitation has been produced using modern technology. It has been demonstrated in the laboratory that the effects of sound vibrations can produce slight levitation. Bell Labs in the U.S.A. produced partial levitation by sound in the 1980s.

In the 19th century, American inventor John Keely, who lived in Pennsylvania, claimed to have levitated metal balls and other objects. He also claimed to be able to disintegrate granite, which contains quartz, a crystal. By causing the quartz to resonate at an extreme rate, it would make the granite break up or disintegrate. This can be compared with some of the research in the King's Chamber, and speculation that the granite there could produce piezoelectric effects (when certain crystals are compressed they produce an electrical field). It is reported that Keely would produce this effect by making his objects out of a combination of copper, gold, platinum, and silver. To produce the levitation, he would blow a sustained note on his trumpet.

THE CORAL CASTLE

Another story involves Edward Leedskalnin, who, in the early twentieth century, built a castle entirely out of large blocks of coral at his home in Florida. Each block weighed between 20 and 30 tons (16,329

RIGHT
Demonstration of magnetic levitation. The photograph shows a small cylindrical magnet floating freely above a specimen of a superconducting ceramic.

RIGHT
Photograph of John Keely (on the right) of Pennsylvania who claimed to be able to levitate objects by blowing a long note on a trumpet.

and 18,143 kg). The completed castle was composed of blocks totaling some 1,100 tons (99,7903 kg) and took him twenty-eight years to complete. He claims to have constructed it all by himself. He never revealed his secret, which he took to the grave. Christopher Dunn, a master craftsman and engineer from Illinois, has investigated this story, known as the "Coral Castle Mystery." Dunn suggests that Leedskalnin had discovered some means of locally reversing the effects of gravity. He also speculates that Leedskalnin generated a radio signal that caused the coral to vibrate at its resonant frequency, and then used an electromagnetic field to flip the magnetic poles of the atoms so that they were in opposition to the Earth's magnetic field.

Does this mean that the Egyptians knew how to employ sonic levitation? All we can say is that from the basic principles of sonic levitation, the structural design of the Great Pyramid (especially the King's Chamber), and from recent research in levitation, the possibility is there.

ABOVE
Is it possible that the builders of this majestic structure had advanced scientific knowledge that allowed them to construct it using some form of levitation?

LEFT
The Coral Castle that Edward Leedskalnin claims to have built entirely on his own. One researcher suggests that he found a way of reversing the effects of gravity and was able to move the heavy stones in this way.

CHAPTER EIGHT

STUDY OF PYRAMIDS

People have always been drawn to the Egyptian pyramids, seeking explanations and answers. One branch of the study of pyramids is known as "pyramidology," which includes the belief that encoded in the measurements of the inner passages of the Great Pyramid are the dates of major historical events. In this chapter we look at some of the theories of the 19th-century pyramidologists.

F irst we will consider an account by a leading pyramidologist, Piazzi Smyth, from his book, *Our Inheritance in the Great Pyramid,* published in 1880. For centuries, the Great Pyramid remained a mystery since no one had been able to penetrate its interior. Then, in 820 CE, Caliph Al Mamoun made a breakthrough, quite literally:

"Caliph Al Mamoun directed his Mohammedan workmen to begin at the middle of the northern side ... Hard labor, therefore, was it to these masons, quarrying with the rude instruments of that barbarous time, into stone-work as solid almost before them as the side of a hill.

"They soon indeed began to cry out, 'Open that wonderful Pyramid! It could not possibly be done!' But the Caliph only replied, 'I will have it most certainly done.' So his followers perforce had to quarry on unceasingly by night and by day. Weeks after weeks, and months too, were consumed in these toilsome exertions; the progress, however, though slow, was so persevering that they had penetrated at length to no less than one hundred feet in depth from the entrance. But by that time becoming thoroughly exhausted ... these murmuring disciples of the Arabian prophet were thus almost becoming openly rebellious, when one day ... they heard a great stone evidently fall in some hollow space within no more than a few feet on one side of them!

"Energetically, however, they instantly pushed on in the direction of the strange noise ... until, breaking through a wall surface, they burst into the hollow way, 'exceedingly dark, dreadful to look at, and difficult to pass' ... No help, however, for the workmen ... So the people tire, but the work

their torches burning low. Then suddenly they emerge into a long tall gallery, of seven times the passage height, but all black as night and in a death-like calm ... while onwards and above them, a continuation of the glorious gallery ... leading them on, as they expected, to the possession of all the treasures of the great ones of antediluvian times ...

"That must surely, thought they, be the high road to fortune and wealth. Up and up its long-ascending floor line ... these determined marauders, with their lurid fire-lights, had to push their dangerous and slippery way for 150 feet [46 m] of distance more; then an obstructing three-foot step [1 m] to climb over ... next a low doorway to bow their heads most humbly beneath; then a hanging portcullis to pass, almost to creep, under, most submissively; then another low doorway, in awful blocks of frowning red granite both on either side, and above and below. But after that, they leaped without further let or hindrance at once into the grand chamber, which was, and is still, the conclusion of everything forming the Great Pyramid's interior ...

"And what find they there, those maddened Muslims in Caliph Al Mamoun's train? A right noble apartment, now called the King's Chamber.

"Ay, ay, no doubt a well-built room, and a handsome one too; but what does it contain? Where is the treasure? The treasure! yes, indeed, where are the promised silver and gold, the jewels and the arms? The plundering fanatics look wildly around them, but can see nothing, not a single dirhem anywhere. They trim their torches, and carry them again and again to every part of that red-walled, flinty hall, but without any better success. Nought but pure, polished red granite, in mighty slabs, looks calmly upon them from every side. The room is clean, garnished too, as it were; and, according to the ideas of its founders, complete and perfectly ready for its visitors, so

goes on; and at last, yes! at last! the ascending passage, beginning just above the granite portcullis, and leading thence upward and to the south, is announced to be free from obstruction and ready for assay. Then, by Allah, they shouted, the treasures of the Great Pyramid, sealed up from the fabulous times of the mighty Ibn Salhouk, and undesecrated, as it was long supposed, by mortal eye during all the intervening thousands of years, lay full in their grasp before them.

"On they rushed, that bearded crew, thirsting for the promised wealth. Up no less than 110 feet [35.5 m] of the steep incline, crouched hands and knees and chin together, through a passage of royally polished white lime-stone, but only 47 inches in height and 41 in breadth [119 by 104 cm], they had painfully to crawl, with

his treasury, and buried by night in a certain spot near the end of his own quarried entrance-hole. Next day he caused the men to dig precisely there, and behold! Although they were only digging in the Pyramid masonry just as they had been doing during so many previous days, yet on this day they found a treasure of gold; and the Caliph ordered it to be counted, and lo! it amounted to the exact sum that had been incurred in the works, neither more nor less. And the Caliph was astonished, and said he could not understand how the Kings of the Pyramid of old, actually before the Deluge, could have known exactly how much money he would have expended in his undertaking; and he was lost in surprise. But as the workmen got paid for their labor, and cared not whose gold they were paid with so long as they did get their wage, they ceased their complaints, and dispersed; while as for the Caliph, he returned to the city, El Fostat, notably subdued, musing on the wonderful events that had happened; and both the Grand Gallery, the King's Chamber, and the 'stone chest without a lid' were troubled by him no more."

long expected, and not arrived yet; for the gross minds who occupy it now, find it all barren; and declare that there is nothing whatever of value, in the whole extent of the apartment ... nothing, except an empty stone chest without a lid.

"The Caliph Al Mamoun was thunderstruck. He had arrived at the very ultimate part of the interior of the Great Pyramid he had so long desired to take possession of; and had now, on at last carrying it by storm, found absolutely nothing that he could make any use of, or saw the smallest value in. So being signally defeated, though a Commander of the Faithful, his people began plotting against him.

"But Al Mamoun was a Caliph of the able day of Eastern rulers for managing mankind; so he had a large sum of money secretly brought from

THE TIME CODE THEORY

In the 1840s, the famous Egyptologist Sir Gardner Wilkinson was the first to dispute the tomb theory of the Great Pyramid. The main evidence he cited was that no mummies have ever been found there, and there is no evidence that a mummy was ever removed or stolen from it.

In the 1990s, another strong argument against the tomb theory was made by Christopher Dunn. Over eighty pyramids have been discovered and explored, and a not a single original burial has ever been found. The granite boxes found in pyramids do not prove there were actually people buried there. Many people do still cling to the tomb theory, but there is little evidence to support it.

Back in 1859, John Taylor of London published the first book on what we now call "pyramidology." This is the belief that the pyramid encodes the dates of major historical events of the world in the measurements of its inner passageways, and Taylor's book marks the beginning of this area of study.

He was the first person to discover that the ratio of the height of the Great Pyramid to the perimeter of its base (the distance around the pyramid) equals the value of pi, just like the ratio of the radius of a circle to its circumference. He believed that the Great Pyramid was built under divine inspiration, an idea that was carried forward by Robert Menzies and Piazzi Smyth. In 1865, Scottish religious

BELOW

The empty Coffer in the King's Chamber. This beautiful granite box was cut from one solid block of chocolate-colored granite, which is even harder than the granite walls of the chamber itself.

The Value of Pi

It is generally accepted that the Greeks discovered the relationship of pi. Pi is the relationship between the radius of a circle and its circumference. The mathematical formula is:

Circumference = 2 x pi x radius (C = 2 x pi x r)

That is, in any size circle you draw, this relationship will always hold true. Thus, if you measure its radius and multiply it by two and pi, this will always equal the circumference of that circle. It appears that the value of pi was built into the Great Pyramid of Giza hundreds of years before the Greeks allegedly discovered it. The vertical height of the pyramid holds the same relationship to the perimeter of its base as the radius of a circle bears to its circumference. If we equate the height of the pyramid to the radius of a circle, then the distance around the pyramid is equal to the circumference of that circle.

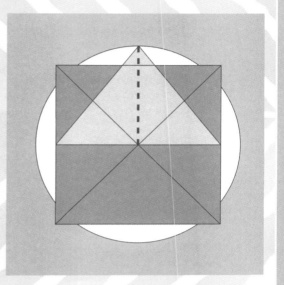

enthusiast Robert Menzies was the first to propose the chronological significance of the passages of the Great Pyramid, which the Edinburgh Professor Piazzi Smyth later took up. In 1864–5, Smyth explored and measured the pyramid in great detail. His books were very popular and brought attention to the Great Pyramid. He first published *Life and Work at the Great Pyramid* in three volumes, and then *Our Inheritance in the Great Pyramid*. He is credited with taking the first photographs inside the pyramid in 1865. He believed the Great Pyramid to be divine.

Smyth also believed that the Coffer in the King's Chamber was a standard of linear and cubic measurement, and that it remained at a constant temperature and barometric pressure. He confirmed Taylor's measurements that the value of pi was built into the pyramid's dimensions. Smyth's measurements also showed that the perimeter was 36,524 pyramid inches, which corresponds to a year of 365.2 days. Thus, the number of days in a year was built into the structure.

REPRESENTING HISTORY

Both Smyth and Menzies believed that the passageway system in the Great Pyramid was a chronological representation of religious and secular events in history. These dates also supported the Bible, and Menzies felt that the pyramid was, in fact, a bible in stone. The basis for this belief is that the various passages were constructed according to a chronological scale of one geometric inch to one year. If we start at a certain point in the Descending Passage that represents a given year, then every inch we move forward represents one year. Major landmarks in the Great Pyramid appeared to correlate with major historical dates.

In order to have a chronology, you must have a starting point. Let us see how this was determined in the Great Pyramid. If we start from the outside of the north entrance and move down the Descending Passage about 40 ft (12 m), we come to a series of so-called "scored lines." These are straight knife-edge lines cut into the blocks from

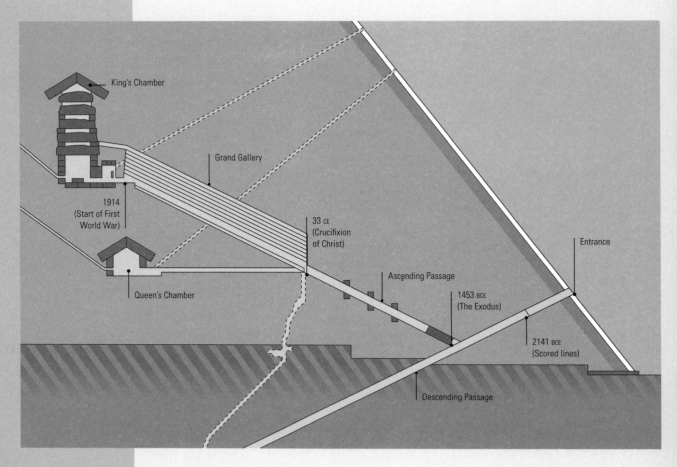

Cross section of the upper part of the Great Pyramid showing the chambers and passageways.

Labels on figure:
- King's Chamber
- Grand Gallery
- 1914 (Start of First World War)
- Queen's Chamber
- 33 CE (Crucifixion of Christ)
- Ascending Passage
- 1453 BCE (The Exodus)
- Entrance
- 2141 BCE (Scored lines)
- Descending Passage

ABOVE

Cross section of the upper part of the Great Pyramid showing the chambers and passageways. There are two systems of passages, a downward, or descending, system and an upward, or ascending, system. According to pyramidologists, major events in human history can be mapped in the configuration of the passageways. The so-called "scored lines" found cut into the stone indicate the beginning of this timeline.

roof to floor. They are on each side of the passage and directly opposite each other. Also, the Descending Passage is in exact alignment to true north. It can be shown that in the last 5,000 years, only once has the North Star lined up exactly with the descending passage and shone directly down it. This occurred in 2141 BCE and the North Star at that time was Draconis, also called the dragon star.

Also only at that time, the star cluster known as the Pleiades in the Taurus constellation was in alignment with the scored lines. Thus, this is what that pyramidologists accept as the starting date of the scored lines. Measurements in inches from the scored lines represent chronology in years. So we count one year for every inch we move from the scored lines, starting at 2141 BCE.

INCHING FORWARD

Now, if we move down the Descending Passage to the beginning of the Ascending Passage, we have moved a distance of 688 inches (17 m). If each inch represents one year, we are at 2141 BCE – 688 = 1453 BCE. This year 1453 BCE is accepted as the date of the exodus of the Israelites from Egypt. It symbolizes now the ascent of man toward God. If we move up the Ascending Passage to a distance of 1,485 inches (37.7 m), we come to the opening of the Grand Gallery. 1453 BCE – 1485 = 33 CE, the year reckoned to be the date of the crucifixion of Jesus Christ. If we travel up the Grand Gallery to its end, we move 1,881 inches (47.7 m). 33 CE – 1881 = 1914 CE, the date of the beginning of the First World War. We can continue moving in the different passages and come up with different dates. Some pyramidologists attempted to predict future events, such as the second coming of Jesus, the millennium, etcetera, but these events did not come to pass.

Why did the pyramidologists choose the inch as the standard unit of measurement? They believed that the linear unit used in the design of the Great Pyramid was the sacred cubit of 25.0265 British inches (63.56 cm). The sacred cubit divided into 25 equal parts results in the sacred inch (also called the pyramid inch), which equals 1.00106 British inches (2.54 cm). Thus the pyramid inch is very close to our standard U.S. geometric inch. The derivation of this unit comes from measurements in the high central section of the King's Chamber passage, called the "Antechamber." It has been found that the length of the Antechamber is equal to the diameter of a circle with a circumference that measures as many pyramid inches as there are days in the solar year, 365.242.

Critics of pyramidology argue that you can find numbers that have meaning in just about anything you measure: if you take enough measurements, you will find what you are looking for.

ABOVE

A painting showing the exodus of the Israelites from Egypt. According to pyramidology, the generally accepted date of this event, 1453 BCE, is encoded within the Great Pyramid, where the Descending Passage meets the Ascending Passage.

The Transit of the North Star

The North Star changes gradually over long periods of time because of the precession of the Earth on its axis (like a spinning top). The orientation of the axis makes a complete revolution over a period of around 26,000 years. Thus we have different North Stars at different times, and sometimes no North Star at all, during this cycle.

LEFT

The star cluster known as the Pleiades. According to pyramidology, the starting point for deciphering the historical events encoded in the Great Pyramid is the scored lines in the Descending Passage, which represent the date 2141 BCE. In this year only, the North Star lined up exactly with the Descending Passage and the Pleiades was in alignment with the scored lines.

Sir Isaac Newton's Study

Not many people know of an obscure work by the famous English scientist Sir Isaac Newton, published posthumously in 1737, entitled: *A Dissertation upon the Sacred Cubit of the Jews and the Cubits of several Nations: in which, from the Dimensions of the Greatest Pyramid, as taken by Mr. John Greaves, the ancient Cubit of Memphis is determined.*

Newton was obsessed with establishing the value of the "cubit" of the ancient Egyptians. His theory of gravity was dependent on an accurate knowledge of the circumference of the Earth. The only figures he originally had were the inaccurate calculations of the Greek geographer and astronomer Eratosthenes. With these figures his theory did not work out. Newton felt that if he could find the exact length of the Egyptian "cubit," this would allow him to find the exact length of their "stadium," reputed by others to bear a relation to a "geographical degree." He believed that this measurement, which he needed for his theory of gravity, was enshrined in the proportions of the Great Pyramid. In 1671, a French astronomer, Jean Picard, accurately measured a degree of latitude to be 69.1 English statute miles (111.2 km). Using these figures, Newton was able to announce his theory of gravity.

ABOVE
Portrait of Sir Isaac Newton. He believed that a measurement he needed for his theory of gravity was enshrined in the proportions of the Great Pyramid.

SCIENTIFIC VALUES

Pyramidologists have discovered many other scientific values in the pyramid. They include the mean density of the Earth, the weight of the Earth, the mean temperature of the Earth, the values of the solar, sidereal (the time for the Earth to complete one revolution of its orbit as measured in a fixed frame of reference, such as a fixed star), and anomalistic years (the time for the Earth to complete one revolution with respect to the extreme points of its orbit), and many others.

OPEN TO THE STARS

In 1883, the British astronomer Richard Proctor put forth his theory and detailed analysis that the Great Pyramid was used as an observatory before its completion. He believed that it could have been used to determine the equinoxes and other astronomical periods and events. The passageways would have been used for lining up stars and planets for observations. The Descending Passage was positioned so that it would have pointed to the North Star at that time, and the Grand Gallery would have been the main place for observations of the stars. He also believed the ramps at the side and holes were used to place moveable seats for people to observe the sky. Again, this would have been before the Great Pyramid was completed and when the Grand Gallery was open to the sky. This idea has cropped up again and again in recent times. One of Napoleon's scientists said:

"It is very remarkable that the opening of pyramids are all to the north. The passage seemed fitted for an observatory, as it formed a true tube, at the mouth of which it would be possible, to see the stars during the day."

PYRAMIDOLOGY PUBLICATIONS

In 1909, two brothers, John and Edgar Morton, explored the Great Pyramid in detail and published their findings with excellent black-and-white photographs in their well-known two-volume work, *Great Pyramid Passages*. They supported the idea of pyramidology and that the pyramid was of divine inspiration.

Adam Rutherford, one of the most famous explorers of and writers on the Great Pyramid in the 20th century, visited the Great Pyramid for the first time in 1925 and made subsequent visits in 1950 and 1963–5. His four-volume set, *Pyramidology*, first published between 1957 and 1972, is considered a classic, full of reference material and photographs. It is one of the best reference sources available. He probably did more to promote the study of pyramidology than anyone else in the 20th century. He explored the pyramid in detail, made some of the most accurate measurements, and took some of the best photographs ever of the interior of the Great Pyramid. His books rank alongside those of Greaves and Vyse as some of the most authoritative and comprehensive.

Another famous 20th-century pyramidologist was the Scottish engineer David Davidson. In 1924 he published his monumental volume, *The Great Pyramid: Its Divine Message*. His book concentrated on chronological prophecy and the detailed mathematics of the Great Pyramid.

SIGNS AND SYMBOLS

In 1936, the founder of the American Rosicrucian Order (AMORC) and Grand Imperator, H. Spencer Lewis, published a book called, *The Symbolic Prophecy of the Great Pyramid*. He proposed that there were numerous underground chambers throughout the Giza Plateau. He believed in the symbolic and ritual importance of the Great Pyramid, and had traveled to Egypt and performed rituals in the King's Chamber.

On one of his visits to the Great Pyramid in the 1920s, with a group of Rosicrucians from all over the world, he performed some supernatural phenomena. No one seems to know the exact nature of his experiments, but many claimed they witnessed such an event. The symbolism of the Great Pyramid plays an important role in Rosicrucian studies and principles.

In the mid-20th century, Edgar Cayce, the well-known psychic and prophet, stated that there was a Hall of Records located somewhere on the Giza Plateau, and that this would be found by the end of the century. Some studies using seismographic equipment have detected chambers or cavities below the paws of the Sphinx. The question remains as to whether these are natural features or are man-made.

CHAPTER NINE

FURTHER THEORIES

The Great Pyramid, with its incredible construction and the precision of the inner chambers and passageways, must have served some purpose. This structure is so unique and the engineering that went into it such an incredible feat that we are led to suppose that it served a higher or more significant purpose than merely being a tomb for a Pharaoh. This chapter discusses further theories as to the purpose of the Great Pyramid and some recent discoveries on the Giza Plateau.

F irst we will explore some of the more recent theories regarding the purpose of the Great Pyramid. They may all be considered to add a piece to the puzzle, but none of them solve it completely.

AN ELECTRIC POWER PLANT

One of the most popular theories belongs to one of our Great Pyramid of Giza Research Association's advisory board members, Christopher Dunn. Mr. Dunn is an engineer and master craftsman. He has measured and analyzed limestone and granite blocks from the Giza plateau and other Egyptian monuments. He argues that we can only explain the great precision of the blocks with some type of advanced machining. The primitive tools and devices that Egyptologists claim the ancient Egyptians would have used could not have cut and polished these limestone and granite blocks with the precision that is seen in the construction of the pyramid. In fact, Dunn finds evidence for ultrasonic drilling in some of the blocks due to the type of bore hole produced. If the stone blocks were worked on using power drilling, then an electrical source must have been available to power the tools. His theory is that the Great Pyramid was used as a device to produce energy to run the power tools of the ancient Egyptians. Thus, it was an electric-power generating plant.

ANCIENT ORAL TRADITIONS

Stephen Meyler, an Egyptologist from Colorado, in collaboration with Egyptian-born indigenous wisdom-keeper, Abd'El Hakim Awyan, substantiate the ancient age of the pyramids. They claim that the pyramids are much older

were never used as tombs. In fact, even academic Egyptologists admit that no intact burial has ever been found in a pyramid in Egypt. It is also interesting to note that the temples were called "Per-Ba," the "house of the spirit," where people went to raise their vibrational level and consciousness. Meyler and Awyan also believe that the Sphinx, known as Tefnut to the ancients, is over 52,000 years old. They claim that the Sphinx is a representation of the primordial mother, built in three stages, with the head carved out of the natural rock first, followed by the front of the body, and finally the hindquarters.

A SACRED SPACE

Robert Bauval, a Belgian engineer, made a very interesting observation in 1983. While watching the stars during a camping trip in Saudi Arabia, he noticed that the Milky Way looked like a river. He also noticed that the three stars in the belt of Orion resembled the orientation and relative size of the three Giza pyramids. In fact, the stars are not perfectly aligned just as the Giza pyramids are not perfectly aligned either. Yet their alignments seemed to resemble each other very closely. He thought the Milky Way resembled the Nile, so he drew a correspondence between these stars and the Giza plateau pyramids. He also pointed out that one of the airshafts in the King's Chamber pointed to the constellation Orion, which the Egyptians associated with Osiris. The airshaft in the Queen's Chamber pointed to Sirius, the star of Isis. Thus he concluded that the Great Pyramid was constructed for ritual purposes, its main purpose being to send the Pharaoh to Orion where he would be transformed into Osiris and live forever.

A TIME CAPSULE

The British author and researcher, Alan F. Alford argues that the subterranean part of the Great Pyramid was a tomb for a king, and that its upper

ABOVE
The three Giza pyramids showing their relationship to the three stars in the belt of Orion.

PREVIOUS PAGE
How the Great Pyramid was built with such exact precision still remains a mystery, but many theories have been proposed.

than academics assert—well over 10,000 years older—and that they used sound to create an anti-gravitational field so the blocks could be lifted with ease. In addition, Meyler and Awyan agree with Christopher Dunn that the pyramids were originally used to produce energy for both practical and spiritual purposes.

The pyramids were called "Per-Neter" by the Ancient Egyptians, which translates as "house of nature." The tombs, on the other hand, were called "Per-Ka," the "house of the body." Meyler and Awyan are both adamant that the pyramids parts served as a sealed repository or time capsule. In his view, the Coffer in the King's Chamber contained meteoritic iron (the seed of the creator-god—the God who, according to the Egyptians, created the universe), whilst the chamber itself generated low-frequency sound that was broadcast to the Giza plateau via its airshafts. The basis for his theory was that the Great Pyramid symbolized and commemorated the creation of the Universe.

A WEAPON

Was the Great Pyramid a weapon, a weapon of mass destruction of extraordinary sophistication and power? That, essentially, is the hypothesis advanced by pyramid researcher Dr. Joseph Farrell. He looked for indications in the ancient texts showing that the Egyptians were aware of such physics that would allow them to develop and use the Great Pyramid as a weapon.

In many instances, he discovered that the ancient texts give a strong impression that the ancients were aware of "zero point energy" or "quantum foam," which recur in modern mathematical models. He also concluded that the basis of the ancients' knowledge of physics was harmonic in nature, and that they must have known about the fundamental constants of quantum mechanics, which would have allowed them to create a weapon out of the Great Pyramid.

Although there is much speculation here, Farrell's theory is one of the more interesting ones regarding the purpose of the Great Pyramid.

FOR VISITORS FROM OUTER SPACE

A unique theory is that of Zecharia Sitchin, who believes the Giza pyramids were built as beacons or ground-markers for visiting aliens. That is, the pyramid would have served as a lighthouse for approaching spacecraft. He is also a proponent of the ancient-astronaut theory (see page 145).

ABOVE
Painting of Osiris, one of the oldest Gods of ancient Egypt.

LEFT
Astronomical photograph of the constellation of Orion. Notice the orientation of the three stars in the belt (center).

Orion
Sirius

Alpha Draconis
Ursa Minor

A SYMBOLIC SPACE

In Chapter 5 we discussed the exploration of the airshafts in the King's and Queen's Chambers. A very interesting theory regarding these shafts has been proposed by Dr. J.J. Hurtak, a well-known archeologist and remote-sensing specialist. He is also an advisory-board member of and special consultant to the Great Pyramid of Giza Research Association.

Dr. Hurtak believes that these mysterious airshafts are aimed at unique star configurations (constellations), possibly for the ascent of the soul towards a particular constellation. From specific star reconstructions, the Southern Airshaft in the King's Chamber can be shown to point to the constellation Orion, and the Northern Airshaft to the constellation Draconis, at a specific date in the past. Thus, by projecting star maps back in time, it appears that the alignment of these airshafts with these specific constellations occurs much earlier than the traditional date of the building of the Great Pyramid (*c.* 2550 BCE, during the Fourth Dynasty). Based on these alignments, Hurtak dates the building to the pre-Dynastic period, which is thousands of years earlier than the Fourth Dynasty.

These calculations for the star alignments reveal that the builders of the Great Pyramid lived more than 4,700 years ago and were so advanced that they were able to use astronomic mathematical equations to create structures and small shafts out of tons of rock and stone. Dr. Hurtak wonders whether they, like the Mayans, were trying to point us to significant astrophysical dates, like building a giant computer calendar or a "chronomonitor." If so, this would make the Great Pyramid the largest astrophysical computer on the planet, although it was built in the ancient world.

Dr. Hurtak also believes that the airshafts pointing to these stellar regions may be equally significant in revealing a special alignment in space of key astronomic locations. Why would the constellation Orion be so important for the Egyptians? They identified Orion with the home of Osiris, the God-King and a symbol of what the ancient philosophers called "the First Principle," the Higher Self. The ancient pyramid texts found on the walls of the tombs tell us, "Orion, the father of the gods, has given a certificate of Life creation as a greater power."

Contemporary astrophysicists have also come to recognize that planet Earth and our solar system exist in a small branch of the Milky Way called the Orion Arm. This may be a clue to a greater evolutionary understanding of our Earth. The constellation Orion seems to be important in some of our modern pyramid research. In Chapter 14, we will see how one scientist has found a strong scientific link between the Great Pyramid and the constellation Orion.

A HIDDEN TOMB

The Great Pyramid is not the only place in which archeologists are searching for hidden chambers. In 1997, a team of researchers, which Dr. Hurtak and his wife Desiree were part of, discovered "The Tomb of Osiris." This tomb was found 100 ft

(30 m) underground and located approximately between the Sphinx and Chephren's Pyramid (the second largest pyramid on the Giza Plateau). The research team discovered this tomb with the use of acoustic signals, seismic readings, and ground-penetrating radar.

The size and scope of the chambers suggest a massive civil engineering project in ancient times. This would have required advanced engineering that could tap into a vast underground series of channels connected to the Nile. The team's research suggests that there may even be additional tunnels behind the walls acting as corridors and connecting every major monument on the Giza Plateau. In time the Egyptian government may grant them permission to continue their exploration of this incredible underground tunnel complex. Who knows what secrets that would uncover?

Besides the possibility of vast underground structures, Dr. Hurtak also believes that the Sphinx itself may be sitting upon a stony ridge protected by a massive underground system of partially dolomitized limestone. This would act as a type of retaining wall beneath it, protecting the structure of the Sphinx from erosion on its eastern side. He suggests that the existence of this possible labyrinth, or vast underground structure, needs to be determined by more remote-sensing technology, followed by excavations and optical cameras. It is hoped that the explorations by Dr. Hurtak and others will unlock the secrets of the Great Pyramid and other structures at Giza.

So, again we have many theories and hypotheses as to the real purpose behind the construction of the Great Pyramid. These modern theories are more varied than the ancient ones, but do they bring us any closer to the truth? More research really needs to be done. The most scientific and credible explanation to be offered so far, in my opinion, is the research of Joe Parr, which will be discussed in Chapter 14. He has put together the greatest body of data and come up with the most comprehensive theory to date.

CHAPTER TEN

POSSIBLE LINKS

Two further theories attempt to explain the purpose of the Great Pyramid. One links it with the Egyptian Book of the Dead, *an ancient collection of religious and magical texts, while another suggests a connection with the Hebrew Ark of the Covenant, which contained the tablets on which the Ten Commandments were written.*

I t has been proposed that the Great Pyramid of Giza is the Egyptian *Book of the Dead* symbolized in stone. This was first proposed by Marsham Adams in 1895. He said that the Egyptian *Book of the Dead* refers to an "ideal structure and to the passages and chambers therein, and that these passages and chambers followed precisely the order and description of those of the Great Pyramid.

"The intimate connection between the secret doctrine of Egypt's most venerated books, and the secret significance of her most venerable monument, seems impossible to separate, and each form illustrates and interpenetrates the other. As we peruse the dark utterances and recognize the mystic allusions of the Book, we seem to stand amid the profound darkness enwrapping the whole interior of the building ... Dimly before our eyes, age after age, the sacred procession of the Egyptian dead moves silently along as they pass to the tribunal of Osiris. In vain do we attempt to trace their footsteps till we enter with them into the Hidden Places and penetrate the secret of the House of Light. [Compare the ancient Egyptian name for the Great Pyramid—"Khut," or "Light."] But no sooner do we tread the chambers of the mysterious Pyramid than the teaching of the Sacred Books seems lit up as with a tongue of flame."

There is another possibility to explain this. The legend holds that there were once writings on the exterior of the Great Pyramid that may have become confused with the writings in the *Book of the Dead*. That is, the ancient Egyptians inscribed their writings not on the pyramid, but on papyrus to preserve them, and this later became the *Book of the Dead*. Is the *Book of the Dead* what remains of this transcribed, corrupted form? Basil Stewart stated in his 1929 publication:

ABOVE AND BELOW
Relief and statue of Thoth,
the Moon-god. The
Egyptians believed that
the ancient collection of
texts known as the *Book
of the Dead* was written
by Thoth.

PREVIOUS PAGE
A detail from the *Book
of the Dead* showing the
Judgement of the Dead.
It has been proposed
that the Great Pyramid of
Giza is the Egyptian
Book of the Dead
symbolized in stone.

"We know that it [the Great Pyramid] contains no such hieroglyphic inscriptions or representations of the heavenly stars and planets such as these traditions infer. It is only when we turn to the *Book of the Dead* that we find the passages and chambers of its 'Secret House' inscribed with such hieroglyphic texts and formulae, and adorned with mythical figures and stars. That is to say, Coptic and Arab traditions have erroneously identified the inscribed passages of the allegorical pyramid in the *Book of the Dead* with the actual passages and chambers of the Great Pyramid itself."

Marsham Adams proposed that the unique system of passages and chambers (particularly the Grand Gallery, obviously unnecessary in a tomb) has an allegorical significance only explained by reference to the Egyptian *Book of the Dead*. The famous Egyptologist Sir Gaston Maspero endorsed his thesis and added: "The Pyramids and the *Book of the Dead* reproduce the same original, the one in words, the other in stone." Can we find meaning in and answers to the mystery of the Great Pyramid by studying the Egyptian *Book of the Dead* and its relationship to the Great Pyramid?

GODLY AUTHOR

What is *The Book of the Dead*? The earliest versions date from the 16th century BCE. The Egyptians believed that it was written by Thoth, the Moon-god, who was also scribe to the gods and responsible for speaking the words of creation. The book is mainly concerned with the state of the departed soul in the afterlife. According to one of the world's experts on the *Book of the Dead*, Sir Wallis Budge, it was not Egyptian in origin but its ideas were brought to Egypt by a different culture that, scholars speculate, was already present prior to the First Dynasty. There has been much theorizing as to who these people may have been, but, in truth, no one knows. We do know, however, that the changes in Egypt at that time were sudden and radical. From a primitive stone-and-flint culture, Egyptian society flowered into one of the greatest civilizations in human history at a speed never before seen, and in a way that has never been repeated. One example of this is the building of the Great Pyramid. The finding of an iron plate within the Great Pyramid that was part of the original structure, suggests the presence of a culture that brought the Iron Age to Egypt at least 2,000 years earlier than scholars had previously thought.

THE GREATEST OF MYSTERIES

The most conspicuous connection between the Great Pyramid and the *Book of the Dead* is that the ancient name for the pyramid is "Khut," meaning "Light." The various stages traversed by the souls of the dead in the *Book of the Dead* are of the deceased going from the light of the Earth to the light of eternal day. It appears that the author, or authors, of the book believed that it contained the greatest of mysteries and was not suitable for just anyone to look at. There is a statement in the *Book of the Dead* that says this book holds a great mystery and should not be made available to the eye of every man; that would be abominable and it should therefore be hidden. The book is concerned with the nature of the Creator and his relationship with his creation, as well as how, and in what ways, mankind is admitted to participate in the mysteries of the Creator. The *Book of the Dead* seems to be almost as mysterious as the Great Pyramid itself. Could there be a hidden code within it which has not yet been discovered?

LEFT
A detail from the *Book of the Dead* from the Tomb of Tuthmosis III (*c.* 1504–1450 BCE) in the Valley of the Kings, Thebes, Egypt.

FAR LEFT
A view of the Grand Gallery looking up. This magnificent hall is 153 ft (42 m) long by 7 ft (2 m) wide at the floor level, rising to a height of 28 ft (8.5 m) in seven courses of polished limestone, each corbeled 3 in (7.5 cm) toward the center. It narrows to 41 in (104 cm) at the top.

ENCODED KNOWLEDGE

There has been much speculation about this original "pyramid" culture. It is also possible that its members left written records of their teachings, and these have come down to us, in a corrupted form, via the *Book of the Dead*. Like any ancient work, it would have been subject to scholars changing and adding elements over time to meet their own beliefs and ideas.

Stewart states: "The allegory contained in the Egyptian *Book of the Dead* is merely a corrupt survival of the allegory enshrined in the Great Pyramid itself." He feels that it was paganized by the ancient Egyptians and applied to their gods. Thus, *The Book of the Dead*, which is a representation of the Great Pyramid, has been corrupted over the years. That is not to say that it is meaningless. It may be possible to filter out the original teaching from the later additions and changes; we could also correlate the *Book of the Dead* with the Great Pyramid to determine where they correspond.

The ultimate goal would be to discover the original teachings of this "common source" and maybe try to identify what they were. It is possible that the knowledge encoded in the

AN EVERLASTING PYRAMID

Marsham Adams proposed an interesting idea in 1895, which was later taken up by Basil Stewart in the 1929 publication, *The Mystery of the Great Pyramid*. He suggested that a very, very ancient "common source" (a person, group, or culture) prior to the ancient Egyptians was responsible for the building of the Great Pyramid. Their purpose in doing so was to enshrine their knowledge and understanding of the mysteries they knew of for future generations. The structure of the Great Pyramid was chosen because it would remain unchanged and uncorrupted over the generations. It would withstand environmental disturbances such as earthquakes or floods, and not be tampered with by man. Written and oral records would not be satisfactory substitutes since they could be changed and edited very easily over time. It would be more difficult to alter and corrupt a large brick structure.

The Great Pyramid is probably an excellent choice to meet the requirements of durability for posterity. Just look at it today. It has been explored, excavated, picked over, and even blasted, but for the most part it is still intact. Thus, the Great Pyramid may enshrine the earliest knowledge of man.

Great Pyramid of Giza is the most ancient that mankind possesses. No assumption is made that this encoded knowledge is correct or is, indeed, the truth. It may simply be a record of very ancient myths, legends, ideas, superstitions, rituals, paganisms, etcetera, that these people believed were true and wanted to preserve. However, any such inherited knowledge would be interesting to us from historical, archeological, and sociological perspectives.

A very useful exercise would be to read the *Book of the Dead* with the structure of the Great Pyramid in mind, and to look for any connections that might come to light.

THE ARK OF THE COVENANT

Many 19th-century researchers of the Great Pyramid pointed out an amazing correlation: the volume, or cubic capacity, of the Coffer in the King's Chamber is exactly the same as that of the Ark of the Covenant, as described in the Bible. Could there have been some common measurement used that goes back thousands of years? Could there have been common builders involved? It has also been shown that the "pyramid inch" (a measurement used in the Great Pyramid) is the same unit of measurement that was used to build Noah's Ark, Solomon's Temple, and possibly the Ark of the Covenant.

In Chapter 1 we talked about the Arab who got the shock of his life on the summit of the Great Pyramid. Is there some kind of electrostatic phenomena on the top of this pyramid? If we go back to ancient legends about the Ark of the Covenant, we find some interesting statements. The Ark of the Covenant was placed in the most "Holy of Holies" and could only be approached once a year by the High Priest. It was considered so sacred that it was believed that if the High Priest, or anyone who came near it, had any impure thoughts, they would be struck dead by a bolt of lightning. A little-known fact is that the Israelites would tie a rope to the leg of the High Priest when he went into the Holy of Holies, in case he was struck by lightning and killed. If that happened, they could just pull him out with the rope and therefore not risk someone else going in and being killed.

When the Nazis approached the Ark in the Indiana Jones movie, *Raiders of the Lost Ark*, they were all struck dead by a bolt of lightning. This scene was based on biblical legend. In the Bible, there is an instance when someone who touched the Ark in order to prevent it from falling was struck dead instantly. Is this biblical reference just mythology, or is there some factual basis to these stories?

ARK AS MACHINE

The Bible says that the Ark of the Covenant was made of acacia wood and lined inside and out with gold. What we have here then are two electrical conductors separated by an insulator. This is a capacitor, a device that can store energy. It has been calculated that the Ark might have been able to act as a capacitor capable of producing an electrical charge of over 500 volts. This could cause the type of phenomena associated with the Ark mentioned in the Bible. Why did the Israelite army always

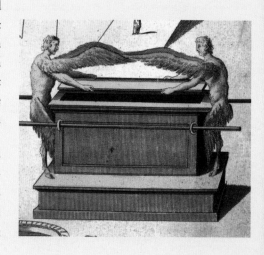

march to war with the Ark in the front? There is much interesting speculation here. Many years ago, the University of Chicago built a replica of the Ark, and it stored an impressive charge. There is an interesting story in the Bible which tells of the Israelites transporting the Ark on a cart, and while turning a corner the Ark starts to tip over. Someone immediately catches it to prevent it from falling to the ground, and his reward is to be killed instantly because he had touched the sacred Ark. He was doing a good deed yet he is rewarded with death. However, if the Ark was a capacitor that gave off a charge that electrocuted him, that would explain what happened.

Why this is important to our subject is that the Great Pyramid may be capable of creating electrostatic effects, especially on the summit. Joe Parr, whose research will be discussed in Chapter 14, actually measured the electrostatic charges on the top of the pyramid and found them to be quite high. Using specific physical apparatus, we believe

it would be useful to take measurements of, and do experiments on, the Great Pyramid, especially at the summit where the capstone would have been. Did the Great Pyramid somehow act as a capacitor and, if so, for what purpose?

PYRAMID TIMELINE

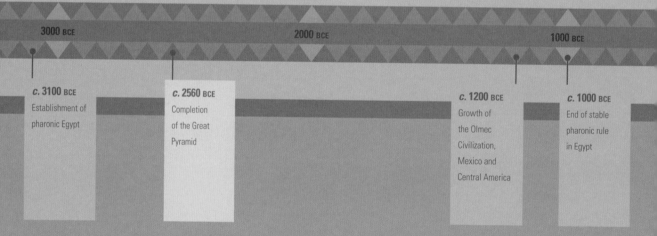

3000 BCE   **2000** BCE   **1000** BCE

c. **3100** BCE
Establishment of
pharonic Egypt

c. **2560** BCE
Completion
of the Great
Pyramid

c. **1200** BCE
Growth of
the Olmec
Civilization,
Mexico and
Central America

c. **1000** BCE
End of stable
pharonic rule
in Egypt

It is very difficult to imagine just how
ancient the Great Pyramid actually is.
This timeline helps to convey this by
showing it in the context of some major
historical events over five millenia.

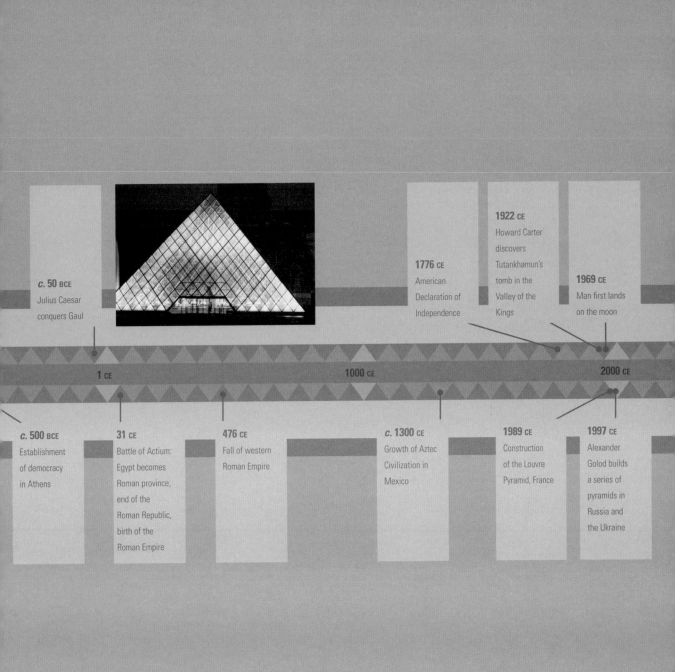

c. 50 BCE
Julius Caesar
conquers Gaul

1776 CE
American
Declaration of
Independence

1922 CE
Howard Carter
discovers
Tutankhamun's
tomb in the
Valley of the
Kings

1969 CE
Man first lands
on the moon

1 CE   1000 CE   2000 CE

c. 500 BCE
Establishment
of democracy
in Athens

31 CE
Battle of Actium:
Egypt becomes
Roman province,
end of the
Roman Republic,
birth of the
Roman Empire

476 CE
Fall of western
Roman Empire

c. 1300 CE
Growth of Aztec
Civilization in
Mexico

1989 CE
Construction
of the Louvre
Pyramid, France

1997 CE
Alexander
Golod builds
a series of
pyramids in
Russia and
the Ukraine

PART THREE   PYRAMID RESEARCH

"Many people are not aware that some
of the largest man-made pyramids were
built in Russia and the Ukraine."

CHAPTER ELEVEN

THE RUSSIAN PYRAMIDS

Most people do not know that some of the largest man-made pyramids in the world were built in Russia and the Ukraine during the last two decades. They were financed and built by a Russian scientist, Alexander Golod, the director of a Russian defense enterprise company in Moscow. Golod had a dream of building large pyramids within which to conduct experiments that he believed would enhance the quality of life on Earth.

Alexander Golod arranged and co-ordinated extensive and detailed experiments within his pyramids, which were conducted by many of the most prestigious research institutes in Russia and the Ukraine. We will explore the results of these incredible experiments in this chapter.

As director of one of the largest research associations studying the Great Pyramid of Giza, I receive a lot of correspondence from people all over the world. In January 2001, Dr. Volodymyr Krasnoholovets from the Institute of Physics in the Ukraine contacted me. (The Institute of Physics was considered the leading military research institute of the former Soviet Union.) This institute helped develop Russian cruise missiles, remote-sensing devices, satellites, space-station technology, and other military technology. Dr. K (as we now call him) identified himself as a senior

scientist at the institute. Over the last ten years he and his colleagues have carried out research inside seventeen large fiberglass pyramids, built in eight different locations in Russia and Ukraine. These pyramids vary in size: the largest is 144 ft (44 m) high and weighs over 55 tons (1,640 kg).

DR. K & ALEXANDER GOLOD
These pyramids are largely unknown outside their respective countries, but they are popular national tourist attractions. Dr. K sent me photographs of these pyramids along with a comprehensive research article that he and his colleagues had written concerning experiments conducted inside them. They asked me to post the article on our Association's website and invited me to collaborate with them. Dr. K explained that Russian and Ukrainian scientists had conducted experiments inside these pyramids, in the fields

of medicine, ecology, agriculture, chemistry, and physics. What is significant about this research is that it scientifically documents the changes to both biological and non-biological materials that have been placed in these pyramids. So I posted Dr. K's article on our website and subsequently, from 2001 to the present, I have appeared on several major radio programs in the U.S.A. and Canada.

Then, in February 2001, Alexander Golod, who actually financed and built the pyramids in Russia and the Ukraine, contacted me directly. Golod, who was a scientist and is now director of a defense enterprise company in Moscow, had found my website, on which I had published Dr. K's research on his pyramids.

Alexander does not speak English, so most of our communications were translated by his son, Anatoli. He told me that his father had started constructing these pyramids in 1989. The Golods also wanted to work with me to help publicize and continue their research. Two months later, I was working with both the builders and some of the major researchers of these pyramids.

ENERGY FIELDS, DESIGN FACTORS

When Alexander Golod was asked why he had built these pyramids, he said that he did so because he was convinced they would be instruments that would benefit humankind. He believed his pyramids would produce an energy field capable of affecting biological and non-biological objects. He even got support from the Russian government for this massive building project, and, in 1998, convinced them to take a kilogram of rocks that had previously been placed in one of his pyramids on board the MIR space station, where they remained for over a year. He believed that the energy fields produced by the rocks would lead to improvements on the space station and possibly back on Earth. Let us now look at these pyramids.

ABOVE

Alexander Golod, the builder of the Russian pyramids, holds a specially made model of one of his structures. These models are based on the exact ratios of the larger pyramids and are filled with a special pyramid matrix that helps produce the pyramid energy fields, just like the larger ones. Golod developed this technology himself.

PREVIOUS PAGE, RIGHT, AND FAR RIGHT

The Russian pyramids are major tourist attractions, and many people, especially over the holidays, flock to spend time inside these structures. Even the cold Russian winter weather does not keep visitors away.

Pyramid Attraction

Everyone wants a photo in front of the largest of the Russian pyramids. People from all over Russia, including government officials, cosmonauts, and even famous actresses, visit this pyramid and spend time inside it. Millions of people have visited it, and, on crowded days, you have to wait in line to enter. Over one New Year's weekend, 20,000 people visited the pyramid in one day.

RIGHT

The famous sketch by
Leonardo Da Vinci known
as "The Vituvian Man." It
was drawn according to the
Golden Section. The design of
the three largest pyramids in
Russia was also based on this
mathematical ratio.

BELOW

A design factor common to
all three pyramids is that they
are hollow inside.

The largest and most recently built pyramid is located about 200 miles (320 km) north-west of Moscow on the Novorizhskoe Highway. It is 144 ft (44 m) high and was completed in 1999. It weighs about 55 tons (1,640 kg) and cost over one million dollars to build. This fiberglass pyramid can be seen from many miles away, and is the main attraction in the area. Many tourists visit the pyramid, and some of the most important of Dr. K's experiments have been conducted within it. The pyramid has a sharper slope (greater acute angle) than the Great Pyramid of Giza. The Great Pyramid has a slope of 51.5 degrees, but the Russian pyramids rise at about a 73-degree angle. Alexander Golod chose this angle based on experimental designs that include the mathematical relationship known as

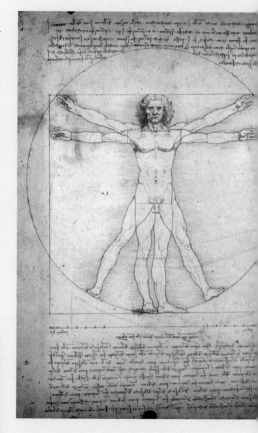

the Golden Section. This is a mathematical ratio on which much of nature is based, as are many works of art and architecture. The ratio is approximately 1.618. Shapes designed using it have always been aesthetically pleasing. Ancient architects were aware of it, and the designs of many of their structures were based upon it.

A design factor common to all of Golod's pyramids is that they are hollow. This was determined following experiments with models before building of the full-scale pyramids commenced. It was also decided that no metal should be included in the structures of these pyramids, as it would interfere with the energy fields. Instead, fiberglass was chosen because it would not interfere with these, and would still be strong enough to withstand the strong winds that occur in and around Moscow.

LEFT
The largest and most recently built of the Russian pyramids is located about 200 miles (320 km) north-west of Moscow. It rises to a height of 144 ft (44 m) and weighs about 55 tons (1,640 kg). It contains no metal within its structure, being composed entirely of fiberglass.

BELOW
The third largest pyramid is exactly a quarter the size of the largest pyramid, being 36 ft (11 m) high. It is located in Romenskoe, a suburb of Moscow. It was one of the first pyramids to be built, and the first in which experiments were carried out.

GOLOD'S OTHER PYRAMIDS

The second largest Russian pyramid is the 72-ft (22-m) structure located about 9 miles (15 km) from Lake Seliger, in the Ostashkov area of the Tver region. It was completed earlier, in June 1997, and is exactly half the size of the largest pyramid. Because the design of these pyramids is based on the Golden Section (see above), this dictates that their sizes will be scaled versions of each other. Thus, the third largest pyramid, which is 36 ft (11 m) high, is exactly one quarter the size of the largest pyramid, and half the size of the second largest. It was built in 1992 and was one of the first pyramids to be constructed. It is located in Romenskoe, a suburb of Moscow. It was here that the first experiments took place.

RIGHT

Notice that the angle of
the slopes of the Russian
pyramids is more acute than
that of the Great Pyramid of
Giza. The Russian pyramids
have a slope of about 73
degrees while the Great
Pyramid has a slope of 51.5
degrees. The dimensions of
the Russian pyramids are
based on the ratio of the
Golden Section.

RIGHT

The second largest Russian
pyramid, near Lake Seliger.
Extinct flowers have started
to grow near this pyramid.

Extinct Flowers

You never know what to expect with these
pyramids. Soon after the construction of
the 72-ft (22-m) pyramid near Lake Seliger,
botanists noticed extinct flowers starting to
grow nearby. This has mystified botanists,
who are unable to provide an explanation.

STRANGE EFFECTS, FUTURE RESEARCH

One of the most interesting observations regarding these pyramids came from Russian Air Force radar. The first indication that the pyramids were producing strange atmospheric effects occurred while the largest pyramid was under construction. It was composed of thirty main layers, or sections, of fiberglass. On the completion of the eleventh section, radar picked up an energy field coming off the pyramid. The nature of this energy has not been determined, but the field was very large and over a mile (1.6 km) high. As construction continued, the energy field remained. When it was completed, a special weather balloon was launched to measure the energy field. The results will be discussed in the next chapter.

Because these pyramids are located in a country with excellent universities, research institutions, and the Russian National Academy of Sciences, valid scientific research can be conducted. It is hoped that this research will be repeated by other scientific institutions around the world in order to verify and validate these findings, as repeatability and peer review are very important factors in science. The scientific community waits

The Earl Lvov Wine Cellar Pyramid

Interest in pyramids in Russia is nothing new; it even goes back to the turn of the 19th century. Indeed, there is a pyramid that was built in the late 1800s, in the Tver region of Russia, as a wine cellar. It is called the Earl Lvov Wine Cellar Pyramid. Supposedly, wine placed in this pyramid tastes better.

LEFT
The Earl Lvov Wine Cellar Pyramid, built in the late 1800s in the Tver region of Russia.

in anticipation for the building of a planned 288-ft (87.8-m) pyramid to see what kind of effects it may produce. Plans are to build it near Moscow, close to the largest pyramid.

LEFT
In 1998 Alexander Golod had special crystals placed in the MIR space station, and they remained on board for over a year. These crystals were originally charged in one of his pyramids, and he believed that their presence on the space station while in orbit would bring benefits both to it and to the Earth.

CHAPTER TWELVE

PYRAMID LABORATORIES

We will now move on to the various types of experiments that were conducted in the pyramids built in Russia and the Ukraine. Numerous scientists and their staff, and some of the most prestigious research institutions in both countries, were involved in these experiments. There has probably never before been such a large, coordinated, and detailed scientific study of pyramids anywhere, and the results have proved extraordinary to say the least.

The research conducted in these large fiberglass pyramids was coordinated and carried out by a number of institutions in Russia and the Ukraine, including the Russian National Academy of Medical Sciences and its affiliate institutes—the Ivanovskii Institute of Virology, the Mechnikov Vaccine Research Institute, and the Russian Institute of Pediatrics, Obstetrics, and Gynecology.

Also involved were: the Institute of Physics in the Ukraine; the Graphite Scientific Research Institute; the Scientific and Technological Institute of Transcription, Translation, and Replication; the Gubkin Moscow Academy of Oil and Gas; and the Institute of Theoretical and Experimental Biophysics. Areas of research included medicine, ecology, agriculture, chemistry, and physics. What is significant is that this may have been the first time that changes brought about by pyramids have been scientifically measured and documented.

PYRAMID EFFECTS

In the 1940s, a Czech inventor drew attention to the effects that model pyramids have on preserving food and sharpening razor blades. This phenomenon was quickly labeled "pyramid power." No one really knew if there was some force or energy field that caused these effects, but the news captured the world's attention. No one at that time could have imagined the type of research that would be carried out inside pyramids in the future. Let us now examine some of the results of these experiments.

1000 Miles

1000 Km

Russia

72 ft (22 m)
pyramid

144 ft (44 m)
pyramid

36 ft (11 m)
pyramid

Moscow

Bashkiria

Kiev

Voronezh

Ukraine

Kazakhstan

Zaporozhye

Astrakhan

Krasnodar

Sochi

Caspian Sea

Uzbekistan

Black Sea

Turkey

IMMUNITY TEST

In 1993, Professor Klimenko and Dr. Nosik at the
Ivanovskii Institute of Virology, which is part of
the Russian Academy of Medical Sciences,
studied the effect of these pyramids
on immunoglobulins—antibodies
that protect us from viral and
bacterial infections. The
researchers took a specific
kind of immunoglobulin
(called venoglobulin) and
placed it in a pyramid for
several days. They wanted to
discover whether the pyramid
would change the ability of this
molecule to help fight harmful viruses in
the body. They then obtained a specific virus
(encephalomyocarditis) from a mouse. They placed
both the immunoglobulin and this virus together
in a culture (a dish with nutrients). They also had

a control group outside the pyramid, containing
immunoglobulins that had *not* been placed in the
pyramid with the mouse virus. The results showed
that the immunoglobulin that had been
placed in the pyramid inhibited
the viruses by more than three
times the control group. This
was a significant result that
could signify the important
potential that pyramids
may have for strengthening
the body's immune system
against infection.

INFECTION CONTROL

To follow up on this experiment, Dr. N.B.
Yegorova at the Mechnikov Vaccine Research
Institute of the Russian National Academy of
Medical Sciences studied the effect of a pyramid on
live animals. She injected mice with specific

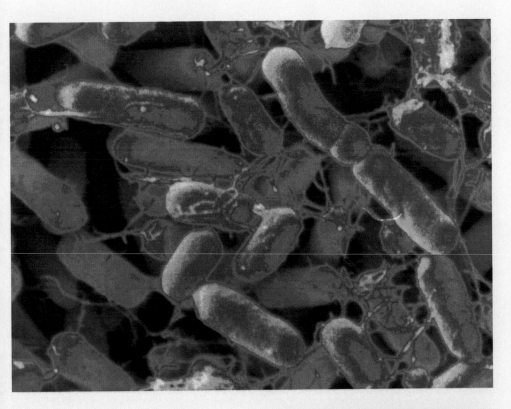

bacteria known as salmonella typhimurium. This bacterium causes a deadly infection, and small quantities are sufficient to kill a mouse. A number of groups of mice were infected with the bacteria and placed in the pyramid for different lengths of time, with the longest being up to a month. Dr. Yegorova also had control groups that were not placed in the pyramid.

Survival rates were recorded for all the groups. Almost all the control animals died by the twenty-fifth day. However, the groups placed in the pyramid had a survival rate of between about 35 and 40 percent, a highly significant result. Remember, several groups were tested, not just one, so this was statistically significant.

Consequently, Dr. Yegorova concludes that the pyramid may have caused changes in cellular and humoral immunities. Both she and her colleagues were very surprised by these results. To get a 35 to 40 percent survival rate with this type of deadly

RIGHT
Many visitors to the Russian
pyramids are interested
mainly in the health benefits
derived from being inside
them. They believe that
the energies produced by
these large pyramids cause
positive healing effects, and
Russian research tends to
substantiate this claim.

Testing for Carcinogens

Surprising results were observed with
mice that had been introduced to different
carcinogens. Some were given water that
had been placed in a pyramid, while other
mice were put in a control group and given
regular water. Swellings for the control group
appeared more often than for those mice that
had been drinking pyramid water.

bacteria is unusual to say the least. The researchers
did their best to keep all factors constant, but
additional studies and research need to be carried
out in order to validate the results.

NEWBORN BABIES

Another medical study was undertaken by a team
from the Russian Institute of Pediatrics, Obstetrics,
and Gynecology, led by Professor A.G. Antonov.
They investigated the influence of solutions of
glucose (simple sugar) on twenty newborn babies
with low indexes (a measurement of the health of a
baby). Some children were given glucose solution

and distilled water that had been placed in the 72-ft (22-m) pyramid; a control group was given ordinary glucose and water. Amazingly, the indexes of all the children given the pyramid-influenced solutions improved far more quickly than those of the control group.

PSYCHIATRIC STUDIES

One psychiatric study involved experiments on 5,000 prisoners in a Russian jail. Certain inmates were administered solutions that had previously been placed in a pyramid. In a short time most violent behavior disappeared within this group as compared with a control group.

Other Russian studies of alcoholics and drug addicts have shown that if the subjects are injected with glucose or given distilled water to drink

Increasing Crop Yields

Over twenty different varieties of seeds were placed in the 39-ft (12-m) pyramid built at Ramenskoe for between one and five days. Thousands of these seeds were then sown outside in a field near the pyramid. The results showed that there was an increase in crop yield of between 20 and 100 percent, depending on the seed. The crops were very healthy and were unaffected by drought.

BELOW
Russian pyramid research has shown that seeds placed in pyramids have a much higher yield than seeds not placed in them. This could have a significant effect on feeding the world's population. More research needs to be done, but the preliminary results are promising.

that has previously been placed in a pyramid, significant improvements are made in combating their addictions. The results show the beneficial effects pyramids may have on mental processes. Again, it is important to emphasize that these are preliminary studies, and more research needs to be done before any widespread application can be attempted. We hope to interest other scientists and researchers from around the world in investigating these fascinating areas of research.

PHYSICAL PHENOMENA

A small group of pyramids were built on an oil-well complex in southern Russia (Bashkiria). After a short period of time, it was observed that the viscosity (thickness) of the oil decreased by 30 percent and the production rate of the wells increased. Chemical analysis showed that the composition of the petroleum (the amount of gums, pyrobitumen, and paraffin) in the oil was altered. The Gubkin Moscow Academy of Oil and Gas confirmed these results.

In 1994, Russian radar picked up some unusual atmospheric effects near the 144-ft (44-m) pyramid north-west of Moscow. Visual observations revealed nothing, but closer inspection revealed a column coming off the pyramid that was several miles high and about half a mile wide. The observers were not sure exactly what it was, but they believed it to be some kind of energy field, the properties of which have yet to be determined.

Using radar again, the Scientific and Technological Institute of Transcription, Translation, and Replication in Kharkiv, Ukraine, then confirmed the presence of what it called an "ionic formation" up to 6,550 ft (2,000 m) above the pyramid and 1,640 ft (500 m) wide. They described this energy field as "ionization of air." An upward flow of the air over the pyramid was also noted.

Several months after the building of this pyramid, Russian environmentalists noticed that a large hole in the ozone layer in the atmosphere above the pyramid was starting to repair itself. Did the energy column coming off this pyramid cause this? It is interesting to note

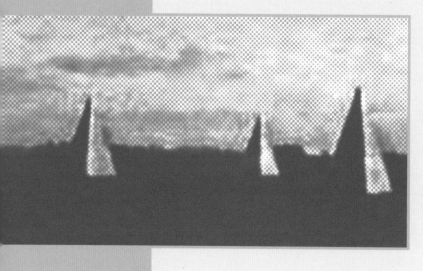

that Alexander Golod predicted this would happen before he even built the pyramid.

Statistics have shown that seismic activity diminishes in areas where pyramids have been built. It has been demonstrated that instead of one powerful earthquake occurring, hundreds of tiny ones take place instead.

In addition, the level of toxicity of substances, including poisons, decreases after being placed inside a pyramid. Radioactive waste also shows a decrease in radioactivity.

MISCELLANEOUS STUDIES

Other experiments included placing distilled water inside a pyramid during three months of winter. The water did not freeze even though the water temperature reached -38 degrees centigrade. When the vessel that contained the water was shaken up, crystallization started and the water quickly turned to ice.

Further experiments have shown that after exposure in a pyramid, the half-life of carbon (the time it takes for unstable carbon 14 atoms to decay to half their amount) was modified, the structure of salt patterns changed, and the optical behavior of crystals was altered.

A group of researchers from the All-Russian Electrotechnical Institute, Moscow, examined the effect of a pyramid on an electrical field. A barrier of rocks that had been placed in a pyramid reduced an electrical charge. Thus, the pyramid showed powerful defensive properties by decreasing an electric discharge and restricting its area.

We will continue the discussion of this research in the following chapter with the findings of the Ukrainian researchers.

CHAPTER THIRTEEN

PYRAMID POWER

Many people have heard about the sharpening of razor blades using model pyramids. This was discovered back in the 1940s by Karl Drbal, a Czech radio technician, and was popularized in the West in 1970 in a book called Psychic Discoveries Behind the Iron Curtain *by Ostrander and Schroeder. Drbal stated that if you placed a razor blade in a miniature pyramid it would stay sharp longer and even resharpen. The force that produced this effect was called "pyramid power."*

Many people believed that pyramids—in this case a model pyramid—generated an unknown field or force that caused these phenomena. It was also thought that food would be preserved longer if placed in a pyramid. These theories were tested by Dr. Volodymyr Krasnoholovets (Dr. K), a theoretical physicist and member of the Institute of Physics in the Ukraine. This institute was one of the top research institutes of the former Soviet Union, and some of its scientists have developed instrumentation for the MIR space station, Soviet spacecraft, and other technologies.

STAYING SHARP

Dr. K placed different brands of razor blades in a model pyramid, which he built using identical rectangular plates of glass. One plate faced west and the other east. Blades were left in the pyramid for thirty days, and a control group that was not placed in the pyramid was assembled. Dr. K was careful to control the effects of differences in air quality, pressure, and other variables in order to minimize any disparity in environment between the two groups. Dr. K, using a scanning electron microscope, then compared the edges of the two sets of blades.

The results showed that there was a significant change in the fine morphological structure (atomic structure of the metal) of the test blades; the so-called "sharpening" of the cutting edge of the razor blades took place only on blades that were placed in the pyramid. Before the experiment was conducted, Dr. K cut out a small segment from each test blade for reference.

LEFT

Model pyramids must be aligned exactly for the sharpening of razor blades to occur.

PREVIOUS PAGE

Dr. Krasnoholovets proposes that the Great Pyramid is a resonator of a special energy field produced by the Earth.

ENERGY FIELDS

Dr. K has demonstrated scientifically that pyramids can affect the structure of metals, in this case razor blades. So, the observation in the 1940s that pyramids sharpen razor blades if oriented correctly within them is borne out.

The big question is, what exactly is this energy field that causes the razor blades to sharpen, and can it be measured? Interestingly, a device called "Tessy," which was developed by a Ukrainian researcher, can possibly measure and map out these energy fields. This device allowed researchers to make a preliminary mapping of the energy field in the Russian pyramids by showing the relative values of this energy. Please bear in mind that these results are preliminary, and further research still needs to be undertaken in order to confirm the measurements.

BELOW

Images of razor blades used in Dr. Krasnoholovets' experiment. The top blade (A) was not placed in a pyramid; the blade below (B) was placed in a pyramid for thirty days.

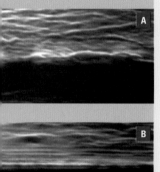

The results of the razor blade experiment are shown in photographs A and B (below left). Fragments placed in the pyramid are compared with fragments from the control group. The control specimen is shown in A, and the segment placed inside the pyramid for thirty days is shown in B. Notice that in A, the edge of the blade looks smooth and not sharp, because it has been used. Thus, there was no change in the edge of the razor blade that had not been placed in the pyramid.

A section of that same razor blade placed in the pyramid for thirty days is shown B. Its edge is coarse, which indicates a sharpening of the blade. Thus, the blade appears to have been sharpened by being exposed to the pyramid. When the whole model was rotated 90 degrees, no distinctions were observed. Thus, the blade has to be correctly oriented for the sharpening effect to occur.

DECIBELS & ZONES

The relative intensity of this energy field is measured in decibels. Below is an indication of how the strength and intensity of the energy field affects humans and animals, according to Dr. K:

• Zones with an intensity up to 3 decibels are considered good and beneficial for most people.

• Zones with an intensity of 3 to 5 decibels may be beneficial for short periods of time, but not for prolonged exposure (over five hours).

• Zones with an intensity of 5 to 7 decibels are very uncomfortable, and people should not expose themselves to this level for more than one hour.

• Zones with an intensity of 7 to 9 decibels are dangerous and harmful.

DISTRIBUTION OF ZONES

Distribution of these zones in the largest Russian pyramid as measured by Dr. K and his colleagues are as follows:

• Towards the very top and above the pyramid— the energy field is very strong and radiates upward. It appears to be around 7 to 11 decibels.

• Below the pyramid—the energy field radiates downward and is over 5 decibels.

• Beyond the pyramid—along the east–west axis the energy is about three times more intense than along the north–south axis.

Dr. K believes that the extreme points of the pyramid (the top, high above it, and below ground level) could be detrimental to humans, although the inside of the pyramid (where people enter) produces positive effects.

Dr. K's results are contrary to the observations of the Russian researchers. According to them, there have been no detrimental effects of the pyramid energy fields.

Thus, more studies are needed to ascertain whether there are indeed negative effects associated with these fields.

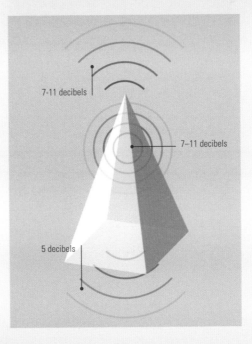

7-11 decibels

7–11 decibels

5 decibels

ABOVE
The largest Russian pyramid. Pyramid energy fields were measured by Dr. K and his colleagues. These were found to vary in intensity throughout the largest pyramid.

LEFT
The energy fields were found to be strongest at the extreme points of the pyramid: at the top, high above it, and underneath it. They also radiated upward.

FAR LEFT
Dr. Krasnoholovets tested the theory that pyramids generate an unknown field or force.

INERTON FIELDS

Dr. K also told us that when the largest Russian pyramid was being constructed, some of the workers high up would lose consciousness, and have to be brought to the ground and moved away from the pyramid. It would be useful to know *what* this energy field is and *why* this happened.

Dr. K believes his discovery of this field means that the Great Pyramid was built intentionally to amplify basic energy fields of the Earth on a subatomic, quantum level (that is, the pyramid energy fields cause changes at the level of atoms and subatomic particles). Thus, these changes occur at the smallest levels of energy and matter as we know them. He calls these fields "inerton" fields, or waves, and he has measured them in model pyramids. According to him, they are fields of the inert force that is also responsible for gravity.

He proposes that the Great Pyramid is a resonator of a special inerton field produced by the Earth. It is a more recently discovered physical field than the electromagnetic or gravitational fields. This field is what affected the materials placed in the pyramids and caused the sharpening of the razor blades.

This inerton field is generated by the friction of moving elementary particles through space. Dr. K does not believe that space is emptiness, as Albert Einstein claimed, but is filled with a substrate, some kind of ether, as scientists in the 19th and early 20th centuries believed. More data has recently come to light to support the presence of this substrate.

THE PARANORMAL

Dr. K believes that Earth atoms vibrate and interact with the ether, thus generating inerton waves. The Great Pyramid concentrates these waves and is saturated with them. These waves then cause the changes in materials. Did the builders of the Great Pyramid know of these waves and construct it as a resonator? Dr. K would like to measure this field in the Great Pyramid to prove his theory that inerton waves spread in a resonator along two mainstream directions, which correspond to the east–west axis and the vertical axis.

Dr. K is also researching the relationship between this inerton field and paranormal phenomena. He believes that all such phenomena may be caused by the presence of the inerton field in nature. This is a very interesting observation, and we will see what his future research reveals.

In the meantime, our researchers are attempting to measure, quantify, and discover what this energy field actually is.

In conclusion, these studies need to be repeated and confirmed by other institutions. We do not advise anyone to attempt them on their own. They should be carried out in a university or institution in which the proper controls are observed. This is one of the main purposes of the International Partnership for Pyramid Research, which I formed with Alexander and Anatoli Golod in 2003.

LEFT
Did the builders of the Great Pyramid know about inerton waves and construct it as a resonator of these?

LEFT
Scientists need to compare the energy fields produced by the Russian pyramids with those of the Giza pyramids.

FAR LEFT
The 144-ft (44-m) pyramid. When this was being constructed, some of the workers near the top would lose consciousness. Was this the result of the energy field?

POTENTIAL APPLICATIONS OF PYRAMID POWER

Anyone looking into Dr. K's pyramid experiments would be amazed at the positive changes in both biological and non-biological materials. If only one-tenth of what the Russians and Ukrainian researchers claim can be verified, then the findings have huge potential benefits for our world. In this section, we will discuss the potential applications of this research, some of which are obvious, some less so.

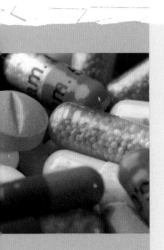

MEDICAL BENEFITS

Pyramids could have a huge impact on healthcare, not only in the U.S.A., which has the best resources to fund such research, but all over the world. The capacity to strengthen the body's immune system against diseases would be a big step toward more widespread preventive medicine. This would not only allow the average person to be more healthy but would also enable sick individuals fighting particular diseases to strengthen their immune system. Also, elderly people, whose immune systems are in decline, could remain healthier for longer and lead more productive lives.

This research could also have very important applications in the health of newborn babies. Veterinary medicine and the care of animals would also benefit. This knowledge could be applied to the global pharmaceutical industry. Pharmaceuticals exposed to the pyramids appear to be more effective and possess fewer side effects.

Our society is not particularly successful in rehabilitating criminals, and exposure to the pyramids could be explored to improve the behavior of individuals who regularly offend. Such exposure could also be useful in controlling and combating drug and alcohol addiction.

We must be very careful here, because we are talking about behavior modification, and this raises important questions. Who determines what good behavior is, and who controls it? These questions need to be asked and the implications explored. Responsibility is an important factor in any experiments in behavior modification.

As mentioned in Chapter 12, Alexander Golod predicted, before he built the pyramid north-west of Moscow in 1999, that the large hole in the ozone layer in northern Russia would repair itself. His prediction proved correct, as the hole began to shrink some months later. The environmental implications are obvious. If we have found a way to repair the ozone layer, this will have extremely positive effects on our environment. If, furthermore, the pyramids can modify our atmosphere and weather to our benefit, we need to pursue such knowledge in depth.

The results of studies on carbon and silicon materials placed in pyramids could have a beneficial impact on computer technology. Due to exposure to the pyramids, changes have appeared to occur in superconducting materials.

Can you imagine the implications for agriculture, especially in countries with low food supplies? The capability to increase crop yields when a limited number of seeds are available would be of great benefit. If seeds exposed to pyramids grow into crops more resistant to drought and pests, this would be an added benefit.

Increase in oil production would help our energy supply. Radioactive waste control would help benefit our environment. In fact, the Golods have

Possible Application of Results

A very important factor to emphasize is that a person does not need to actually be inside a pyramid for these results to occur. Drinking water placed in the pyramids also seems to produce the desired effects. Thus, this water could be brought to others who have not been able to visit the pyramids. In addition, as seen with the studies of newborn babies, both water and glucose solutions administered to them produced beneficial results without them going inside the pyramids.

Bottles of water and glucose solutions that have been placed inside pyramids could be mass-produced and then exported to other countries and distributed by reliable sources, all quite inexpensively. Of course, there need to be regulations and controls, and this raises a whole set of issues beyond the scope of this book. Currently, when you visit the pyramids in Russia, you can take home bottles of water that have been placed in them for days or weeks, so this application is happening right now. We still need to carry out some important experiments to determine how the pyramids affect the solutions being placed in them. We also need to determine how much the pyramids increase the effectiveness of the solutions, and whether the length of time the solutions spend in the pyramid is an important factor. These relationships need to be qualified and quantified.

suggested using model pyramids in the Chernobyl submarines, which use nuclear power, to minimize the toxicity of the nuclear waste produced.

CONCLUSIONS

It appears that the Russian and Ukrainian scientists have demonstrated that these pyramids do affect biological and non-biological materials. It is extremely important to conduct more tests because, as mentioned before, independent verification is essential. That is one of the purposes of the International Partnership for Pyramid Research, a collaboration of pyramid research between our Great Pyramid of Giza Research Association, and Alexander and Anatoli Golod.

It is important to emphasize that this research, which has cost millions of dollars, was a coordinated program that included at least eight major academic and industrial institutes and over a dozen researchers of repute and their staff, so it is to be taken seriously.

BELOW
Many have built pyramids to meditate in and experience their effects.

CHAPTER FOURTEEN

HYPERSPACE ADVENTURES

If another researcher were to brief me on the findings that I am about to discuss, I would be very skeptical, and my first question would be: Who did this research, and what are his or her credentials? So, for this reason, I want first of all to tell you a little about Joe Parr.

I first met Joe Parr several years ago. He has been an electronics engineer for over forty years, and he recently retired from employment with a company that develops deep-sea oceanography transducers in California. He is known as the inventor of the gamma ray transducer, which is a device for measuring levels of radioactivity around different energy sources. He was also involved in eight government projects spanning the globe, including the Arctic and Antarctic, where he wintered. So this is a man with excellent credentials and an extensive research background.

He is also one of the few people to have spent an entire night on two separate occasions (first in 1977 and again in 1987) on top of the Great Pyramid of Giza, conducting a range of electrical, magnetic, and radioactive measurements.

An interesting story is that, in the 1960s, he hired Dr. David Virmani to help set up a research facility in Las Vegas. Previously, Dr. Virmani developed and installed a secret communications system for Juan Peron, the former Argentinian dictator. Its purpose was to enable Peron to keep in contact with his generals without being overheard. This new type of polyphasic communication was so successful that Peron distrusted anybody who knew about it and ordered his men to take Dr. Virmani out into the desert and eliminate him. Fortunately, he escaped and continued his research with Joe Parr, developing polyphasic communication systems, and experiments in bouncing signals off the moon. The latter they achieved using a very large antenna and transmitting a radio frequency burst.

This led Joe Parr to conduct research into rotating pyramids, magnets, and radioactive sources. He has now been involved in pyramid research for over thirty years and is currently Research Director of the Great Pyramid of Giza Research Association. Let us now look at the experiments that he has been doing with model pyramids in his laboratory.

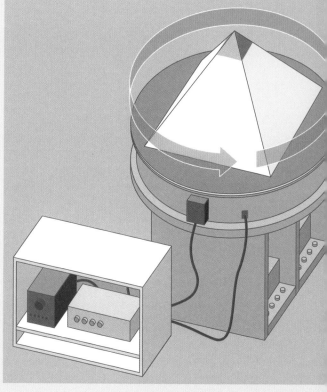

Like some of the early pyramid researchers, Parr found that strange physical phenomena happen inside any object in the shape of a pyramid. Other shapes—such as cubes, octagons, and spheres—do not cause the same phenomena.

Parr has uncovered and measured a low-level energy field that forms around pyramids. Both small pyramids and large ones, such as the Great Pyramid, are surrounded by this energy field. He calls it a bubble, or orb. We do not yet know why this field forms around pyramids, but we do know that it can be strengthened or weakened by other kinds of energy or forces. A resting pyramid, or a pyramid without motion, has this bubble or energy field around it, but it is not very strong and varies over time. In fact, the energy field is not always present and at times seems to disappear.

Since the energy field is not always present, and is not very strong when it is, Parr developed an elaborate experimental set-up. He discovered that by rotating a model pyramid in an alternating magnetic field, he could increase the pyramid's energy field so as to be able to measure it and study its effects. This was accomplished by creating a high-speed centrifuge with a pyramid mounted at the end of one of its arms, which was then spun at very high speeds (950–1,800 rpm) through a magnetic field.

THE BUBBLE AS SHIELD

During these experiments, Parr discovered that this bubble acts as a shield that can block out all known types of electromagnetic radiation, even gamma rays. The more energetic the bubble becomes, the greater its attenuation and blocking, or shielding, effect. In fact, when the bubble is fully energized, it completely blocks out all known forces and electromagnetic fields. Parr placed radio-frequency sources, radioactive sources, and ion sources inside the pyramid and measured the amount of blocking caused by the bubble.

LEFT
A model pyramid next to the high-speed centrifuge.

BELOW
Only the pyramid shape produces a bubble around it in Joe Parr's experiments. Other shapes, including cubes, spheres, and octagons, do not.

RIGHT
Joe Parr on the summit of the
Great Pyramid in May, 1987,
with Chephren's pyramid in
the background.

FAR RIGHT
Besides the energy bubble
surrounding model pyramids,
an energy field also envelopes
larger pyramids, including the
Great Pyramid of Giza.

WEIGHTLESSNESS

Another experiment performed by Parr was to examine the effect of gravity inside the bubble by measuring the weight loss of objects placed inside the model pyramid. He used an Ohaus Precision Plus scale, an extremely sensitive weight-measuring device. He discovered that not only did the bubble completely block all other known energy fields, but that objects lost weight when inside the bubble. Gravitational pull, which obviously acted on the pyramid before, was reduced because of the shielding effect of the bubble.

Parr has demonstrated that this bubble does indeed block off all other known energy fields. Now a strange thing happens. Not only does the bubble partially block these other energy sources, but at certain times of the year it completely closes off to all known forces (gravitational, electromagnetic, radioactive, etcetera) and objects inside the model pyramid become weightless. The pyramid tears off the machine arm of the high-speed centrifuge and is propelled into space. It flies off as if it wants to move in a specific direction. Parr has performed over fifty-five experiments that seem to indicate that at that moment the pyramid can pass through other physical objects. Parr thinks that it does not then occupy the same physical space but exists in another spatial dimension, which we call hyperspace. We live in a three-dimensional spatial world (length, width, height), and hyperspace is the fourth spatial dimension.

A CONDUIT TO ORION

One of the times of year during which this phenomenon happens is from December 13–16. At this time the Earth passes between the Sun and the constellation of Orion. Parr has discovered an energy conduit between the Sun and Orion, and the Earth passes through this conduit—which consists of a stream of neutrino particles coming from the Sun—in mid-December. It appears that the conduit energizes the bubble and closes it off to all other energy forces. An interesting correlation is that the Southern Airshaft in the King's Chamber of the Great Pyramid of Giza points towards the constellation of Orion.

Dan Davidson, an independent researcher from Arizona, has repeated some of Parr's experiments, and he arrives at almost the same conclusions. Dan thinks that when the bubble closes off to all known forces, the model pyramid starts moving, gathering energy very rapidly, and proceeds to travel down this energy conduit. It rips off the centrifuge because it is trying to move in this conduit towards Orion.

Parr has also found that this bubble can be energized and turned on and off with sound. He has discovered the resonant frequency of

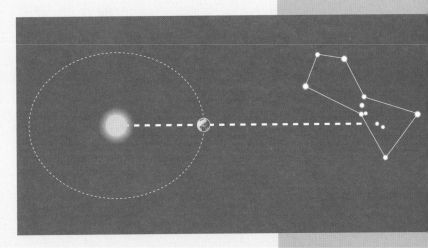

the bubble to be 51.5 cycles per second (Hz); the slope of the Great Pyramid is 51.5 degrees. Is it a coincidence that the angle of the pyramid is numerically the same as the resonant frequency of the pyramid's force field? I do not believe that it is. The builders of the Great Pyramid knew something that we do not.

ABOVE
A diagram showing the alignment of the Sun, the Earth, and the constellation Orion. The stream of neutrino particles in the conduit discovered by Joe Parr is indicated by dashes.

THE GREAT ANNIHILATOR

Was the Great Pyramid built specifically as a device to travel to the constellation of Orion? Could this energy conduit be a communications device or a star-gate (a channel connecting distant regions in space for instant movement between them) between Orion and Earth? This brings us to another interesting observation by Joe Parr.

30° Longitude from Greenwich

The Great Pyramid

30°

North Latitude

Equator

Parr noted in his log book that toward the end of 1979 and into 1980 the bubble, or energy fields, on stationary pyramids disappeared. He had no idea why this happened. Then, several years later, the bubbles came back. It was not until 1990 that he discovered the answer.

GAMMA-RAY SOURCE

In 1979, using a weather balloon, astronomers discovered something located in the center of our Milky Way galaxy (25,000 light years away) that they called the "Great Annihilator." This is a powerful, high-energy gamma-ray source. Gamma rays contain more energy than any other wave in the electromagnetic spectrum, and high levels can kill all living things. No one really knows for sure what this Great Annihilator is, nor what it is doing, but some speculate that it is a black hole or two black holes circling one another.

NASA later also detected and confirmed the existence of this Great Annihilator. In the spring of 1980, the gamma-ray source was diminishing, and it appeared to be going away. Then, in 1988, the source was picked up loud and clear again. So it comes on and goes off at different times, as Parr had already noted.

When the Great Annihilator emitted gamma rays, the bubble around the pyramid started up; when it stopped, the bubble disappeared. So, it seems that the Great Annihilator located in the center of our galaxy is controlling the energy field around the pyramids.

AT THE CENTER OF THE EARTH

The Great Pyramid was built at a latitude of 30 degrees north (30 degrees, 58 minutes, 51.06 seconds) and a longitude of 31 degrees east (31 degrees, 9 minutes, 0.0 seconds). People have been discussing and debating this since the 1800s when Piazzi Smyth, the great explorer and pyramid researcher, discovered that this location is the "center of the land mass of the earth." That is, at this location the lines of latitude and longitude cross more of the Earth's land mass than at any other location. Another way of looking at this is that these lines of latitude and longitude that intersect at the pyramid's location divide the Earth's land mass into roughly equal quarters.

But Parr has recently found a more important reason for the location of the Great Pyramid. It was built at 30 degrees north because at that location its base would point once a day exactly toward the galactic center (a line drawn through the center of the pyramid and continuing through the Earth would point directly to the galactic center once a day). This only happens at the 30-degree parallel. We will now look at why this is important to Parr's research.

LEFT
Astronomical photograph of the Great Annihilator. This was discovered by astronomers in 1979 at the center of our galaxy. The gamma rays emitted by the Great Annihilator appear to control the energy field around the pyramids.

SHIELDING THE EARTH

Joe Parr's work puts together much of the information and scientific knowledge we have relating to the Great Pyramid. His scientific approach, and the repeatability of the experiments, lends much credibility to his work. His research may help solve the puzzle of why the Great Pyramid was built. A summary of the results leads to another interesting theory.

THE FACTS SO FAR

Here is a summary of what we know so far from Joe Parr's research:

1) We know that the energy field, or bubble, around the Great Pyramid is connected to the gamma rays given off by the Great Annihilator. When the gamma rays are not emitted, the bubble disappears; when they are emitted, the bubble forms again.

2) We also know that the base of the Great Pyramid faces the galactic center once each day. This only happens at a latitude of 30 degrees north.

Is the pyramid monitoring the galactic center and the amount of gamma rays that are emitted?

3) We know that the bubble acts as a shield, which blocks off all known types of radiation including gamma rays. The purpose of a shield is to protect something. Maybe the pyramids of Egypt were built to protect the world from a deadly burst of gamma rays from the Great Annihilator. Will this shield come into play automatically when the gamma ray levels exceed a certain point? Or will humans have to play a part? What about the

BELOW

The Nubian pyramids in Sudan. Is it possible that pyramids were built around the world to protect the Earth from destruction by a high-level burst of gamma rays?

capstone from the Great Pyramid that is missing or was never there? Is this an integral part of the shield's apparatus that will need to be found and put in place?

Scientists at NASA and the University of Kansas, U.S.A., have reported that hundreds of millions of years ago a mass extinction on Earth could have been triggered by a star explosion called a gamma ray burst. Is it possible that whoever built the Great Pyramid, and maybe other pyramids the world over, knew that sometime in the future the galactic center would emit a deadly pulse of gamma rays that would destroy human life on Earth?

The question is how large could the protective bubble be? Is it just localized around the Great Pyramid and thus able to shield only those lucky enough to be in the vicinity at the time? Or could the bubble expand, and surround and protect the entire globe and everything living on it?

LEFT
A step pyramid at Tikal, Guatemala. Could the builders of pyramids all over the world have known that at some point in the future human life on Earth would be destroyed by a deadly emission of gamma rays?

ENERGY BUBBLES AND HONEY BEES

About five years ago, a very large energy bubble was produced in Parr's research lab that filled the surrounding area. It has varied in size over the years—it was originally about 100 ft (30.4 m) in diameter, but has shrunk at times to 25 ft (7.6 m)—but he cannot get rid of it, no matter what he does. He is not sure, but it seems to be an expansion of the smaller experimental bubble that formed around his model pyramids when spun in the centrifuge. Parr measured the pressure both inside and outside this bubble, but the difference was very small at around 1.5 pascals (Pa).

An interesting effect of this large bubble occurs when honey bees chance upon it as they look for flowers. Immediately on entering the bubble the bees lose their navigational abilities. They cannot walk straight or fly, and are able to move their wings only. They die within a few hours.

Could this discovery be related to the recent reports that have come from at least twenty-two states in the U.S.A. of unusual bee-colony deaths? Bee-keepers have reported losing more than 50 percent of their bees, often with just a handful of worker bees surviving.

About ninety crops in total—including fruits, vegetables, and almonds—depend on bees for pollination. Without honey bees to pollinate these crops, the impact on food production and global economics could be disastrous.

Researchers are scrambling to find the reason for this decline in honey bee numbers, which is called "Colony Collapse Disorder." Possible causes that have been suggested include genetically modified crops, mites, pathogens, pesticides, and even electromagnetic radiation from cell phones. But the definitive cause is still unknown.

Most recently, a team of scientists from Edgewood Chemical Biological Center and the University of California, San Francisco, identified both a virus and a parasite that are likely causes of this decline, but not everyone concurs.

In 2007, an entomologist at the University of Illinois said that the bigger mystery is why bees are not returning to their hives. If worker bees do not return to the hives they cannot communicate the location of flowers and other plants. If this happens, the colonies die. Is something affecting the bees' navigational systems? Perhaps Joe Parr's research could shed some light on this.

RIGHT

An almond tree. About ninety crops, including almonds, depend on honey bees for pollination. Could the pyramid energy bubbles be related to recent unexplained bee-colony deaths in several states around the U.S.A.?

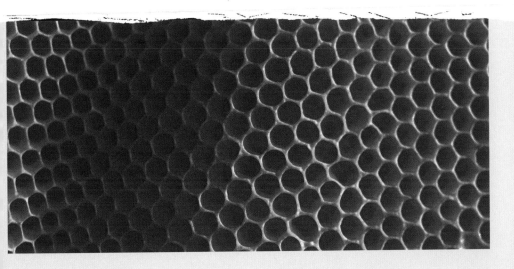

LEFT
It is a mystery why, in some parts of the U.S.A., honey bees are not returning to their hives, and therefore not communicating the location of flowers and other plants. Could Joe Parr's research provide some answers?

WING VIBRATIONS

In flight, a bee's wings vibrate at around 200 cycles per second (cps). They produce a high-frequency hum that you can hear. Joe Parr set up an audio oscillator at 200 cps and ran it in the lab for twenty-four hours a day to see whether this would cause more bees to come into the bubble and what effect this would have on those entering it. When he ran this audio oscillator, both he and his wife became disoriented quite frequently. They would walk into a room and ask themselves, "Why did I come here?" When the oscillator was turned off, their disorientation disappeared and they returned to normal.

Now, if you play an audio frequency of 200 cps by itself, this will not cause disorientation. But in Parr's lab this frequency was interacting with the energy bubble, and together they produced the effect of disorientation that Parr and his wife were experiencing. We believe that the bees' hum of 200 cps interacts with the pyramid's energy field to produce disorientation. Do you need to hear it to become disoriented? We do not know for sure, but whether you physically hear it, or whether it vibrates or resonates with something in your body—or the bee's body—it produces the effect of disorientation.

Parr believes that this bubble, or energy field, is not user-friendly at specific times of the year, and that this is dependent on the sun's eleven-year cycle. During particular times of the year, Parr has discovered that the bubble can extract energy from any source, either mechanical or biological. Therefore, he believes that meditating inside a pyramid at these times is not to be recommended, as preliminary evidence shows that extended exposure to the bubble may cause interference with higher brain functions.

IMPLICATIONS OF RESULTS

Parr's results could have significant implications for space travel and maybe even time travel. Let us explore some of these possibilities.

If objects inside the bubble lose their weight, perhaps this effect could be applied to levitation and moving large objects. The shielding property of the bubble could also have military applications. Can you imagine a soldier, or even an entire country, having this kind of shield?

Finally, if pyramids move down the energy conduit between the Sun and the constellation of Orion, there might be potential for a new transportation system in space. But first many more studies need to be conducted.

CENTER
Joe Parr has discovered that when honey bees fly into the large energy bubble inside, and surrounding, his lab, they lose their navigational abilities and eventually die.

BELOW
Astronomical photograph of the sun showing sunspots. The number of sunspots visible waxes and wanes as part of the sun's eleven-year cycle. Joe Parr's research indicates that at certain times of the year, dependent on this cycle, the pyramid energy bubble may not be user-friendly.

CHAPTER FIFTEEN

PYRAMID SCIENCE

We have now entered a period of pyramid studies in which we are using rigorous science to analyze and quantify pyramid power. Let's first look at the beginnings of pyramid power in the past century.

A French inventor, Antoine Bovis, visited the Great Pyramid of Giza in the 1930s. In the King's Chamber he noticed a dead cat and mouse. These animals showed no signs of decay but were desiccated and appeared mummified. Back in France, he decided to build some cardboard model pyramids and perform an experiment. He realized that orientation was crucial and so oriented his model pyramids in the north–south direction, exactly like the Great Pyramid. He placed a small stand inside the pyramid one-third the way up, just like the location of the King's Chamber in the Great Pyramid. He placed raw meat on this platform and left it for several days. During that time, it should have become rotten, but when he checked it, he noticed that it had become desiccated without rotting. This proved to be one of the first modern experiments into pyramid power.

John Hall, a researcher from the U.S.A., carried out experiments with model pyramids in 1935. Using a copper ring and wires, he showed that an electrical charge was emitted from the apex of the model pyramid. In the 1940s, Karl Drbal, a Czech radio technician, read about Bovis's experiments. He repeated many of them in the 1950s and achieved the same results. He was the first to place a razor blade in a model pyramid one-third of the way up, and then to examine it some time later. He discovered that dull razor blades became sharper in the pyramid if the cutting edge of the blade was oriented in the correct direction (north–south). Instead of getting only a few shaves out of these blades, he could get fifty or more, because the blades maintained their sharpness in the pyramid. Drbal applied for a patent for his model pyramid, which would allow razor blades to retain their sharpness. He received it in 1959.

BIOCOSMIC ENERGY

Years later, a brilliant researcher from the U.S.A.,
Dr. Patrick Flanagan, also undertook experiments
with model pyramids. As one of the first people to
study pyramid power scientifically, he published
the first book on this subject in 1973, called
Pyramid Power. He wanted to identify the energy
that was emitted, or produced, by objects that
were in the shape of a pyramid. He went to Egypt
over thirty times and believed there was energy
coming from the Great Pyramid of Giza, which
he called "biocosmic energy." He also verified the
experiments of Bovis and Drbal, and showed that
raw meat placed in model pyramids would not rot
but became desiccated and mummified.

Dr. Flanagan believed that this energy has its
greatest concentration in the King's Chamber
(see Chapter 16), which is located about one-
third of the way from the top of the pyramid. He
performed experiments with other shapes but
they did not reproduce the same level of energy.

Thus the pyramid's unique shape was the cause
of biocosmic energy. Dr. Flanagan continues
to investigate the effect of pyramids, and his
research into this energy has also focused on
electromagnetic energy, Kirlian photography,
and other techniques. Kirlian photography uses
high-voltage discharges that some believe can
photograph the human aura and the auras of all
living things. It produces a corona discharge which
is captured on photographic film, and many believe
that this is the image of the spiritual life force, or
energy, of living matter. Dr. Flanagan goes down
in history as one of the first to carry out pyramid
research scientifically.

RECENT RESEARCH

More recently, Dr. Krasnoholovets from the
Ukraine has continued to research pyramid power
and has performed electron microscope scans
of the razor blade experiment, from which he
claims to have identified this pyramid energy field
(see Chapter 11).

Also, as was shown in Chapters 11 and 12,
the Russian and Ukrainian researchers have
demonstrated that pyramids can affect both
animate and inanimate objects. The Russian
research shows the health benefits that pyramids
produce, and that they can also affect the mental
states of individuals.

Joe Parr (see Chapter 14) has also produced preliminary data suggesting that the pyramid shape and its energy field (or bubble) can cause changes in brain function.

A Canadian researcher and inventor, Edward Gorouvein, formerly from Russia, has worked with Alexander Golod (see Chapter 11) for many years and is developing pyramid products (model pyramids, crystal pyramids, and the building of larger pyramids) to try to utilize the energy fields produced by the Russian pyramids. He has had a good deal of success applying his ideas and products in health clinics, and with practitioners in Canada. Currently he is working with architects to design and develop pyramidal houses based on the Russian pyramids.

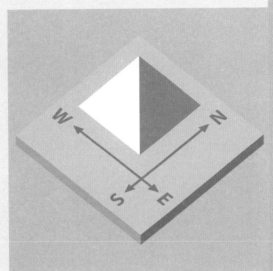

PHARAOHS' RODS

On some statues and drawings from ancient Egypt, Pharaohs can be seen holding long cylindrical rods. No one knows for sure what these rods are, nor what purpose they served. Russian researchers Svetlana and Sergey Gorbunovy have looked into old records and manuscripts, and have reproduced replicas of these rods as they can best conceive them and their purpose. The rods they manufacture are hollow cylinders made of copper (for the right hand) and zinc (for the left hand), with a special filling inserted into each type, based on descriptions from old manuscripts. These fillings vary and can contain quartz crystals, metals such as iron or zinc, or even fluids. Before being inserted into the rods, these fillings are placed in the largest Russian pyramid for twelve days. This supposedly provides molecular and energetic enhancement. Many people have used these rods for medical and spiritual purposes and they are very popular with Russian alternative health practitioners. People have claimed that the rods enhance memory, intuition, and the immune system, that they harmonize the body, and reduce stress and fatigue.

PYRAMIDS AS ANTENNAE

Kirti Betai, an advisory board member to the Great
Pyramid of Giza Research Association, and an
alternative health practitioner from India, has used
pyramids to treat over 50,000 patients in the last
eleven years. He claims that the Great Pyramid of
Giza and other pyramids built across the world were
designed to insulate the mummified body from
interactions with the surrounding environment,
and thereby prevent decay.

Betai believes that the pyramid shape behaves
like a unique antenna, which attracts, accumulates,
and accelerates geological, biological, and cosmic
energy particles from its own environment, just as
television and radio antennae, which are made from
similar materials, attract different signals because
of their unique geometric shapes. Pyramids made
from different materials, geometric shapes and
sizes, and placed in different locations, attract varied
energy particles from their energy environments,
and therefore their energy force fields have their
own unique properties. Pyramids made from the
same materials, of the same size and shape, will
acquire different energy spectrums depending
on where they are erected; they would also have
different properties.

MEDITATING IN PYRAMIDS

It is also claimed that people have received
beneficial effects by meditating within, under,
or near pyramid shapes. Some have claimed
that pyramids can produce altered states
of consciousness and out-of-body experiences.
All these claims need to be carefully verified
scientifically, but it appears that they can be
substantiated, and it also seems likely that the
ancient Egyptians were aware of these effects.

There are several important large contemporary
pyramid structures that have been built around
the world for the purposes of meditation. The
largest and most interesting is the pyramid at
the Osho Meditation Resort in Pune, India,
which opened in November 2002. This pyramid
is approximately nine storeys high (about 131 ft
or 40 m) and is composed of steel and concrete. It
took about four years to complete and can hold
over 5,000 people. It was designed especially for
meditation by an Indian mystic and spiritual
teacher known as Osho, who gave instructions
for it to be built after his death (he died in 1990).
Many other spiritual teachers and mystics from
India have acknowledged the power of the pyramid
shape for meditation.

PYRAMIDS IN ITALY

In May 2003, an article entitled, "Le tre piramidi di Montevecchia" was published by Cinzia Montagna on an Italian website (www.lombardiainrete.it) about a satellite image that had captured three ancient pyramids in northern Italy, in the town of Montevecchia. They look like hills because they are covered with vegetation, but they appear to be 500 ft (152.4 m) high and made of stone. Their slopes are about 42 degrees and appear to be aligned with the constellation of Orion since they match the three stars in Orion's belt. The age of the pyramids has not yet been determined but initial assessments put them at over 3,000 years old. It will be interesting to see what these pyramids reveal when they are uncovered and explored.

Besides the well-known Egyptian and Mexican pyramids, ancient pyramids have been discovered more recently in China, Bosnia, Ireland, Italy, and other places around the world.

SCIENTIFIC CONCLUSIONS

Since pyramid power in modern times was first observed and studied by Antoine Bovis in the 1930s, researchers continue to the present day to learn more about these intriguing energy fields. It is perhaps not quite as mysterious as before, because science is having some success in quantifying and identifying the inherent energies. We do not have absolute answers yet, but we are coming ever closer to them. With the continuing work of the Russian and Ukrainian researchers, more is bound to be revealed.

CHAPTER SIXTEEN

FINAL REFLECTIONS

Why have so many people been drawn to the Great Pyramid of Giza throughout the ages? Is it the romance of Ancient Egypt or something less specific that speaks to the unconscious?

The reasons are numerous. Many people study the Great Pyramid of Giza from a purely academic perspective driven by an intellectual curiosity. They may be archeologists, historians, scientists, mathematicians, or other professionals who are drawn to study the Great Pyramid as it relates to their chosen discipline.

UNIVERSAL APPEAL

It seems many others, who are not studying the Great Pyramid from an academic standpoint, are drawn to it by some less identifiable response. Throughout history, the Great Pyramid has fascinated many well-known historical figures. As we have seen, both Alexander the Great and Napoleon visited the Great Pyramid. Napoleon even spent time alone in the King's Chamber (see Chapter 3). Sir Isaac Newton was extremely interested in the Great Pyramid and thought he could discover certain mathematical values from it that would help him prove his theory of gravity. He even wrote a dissertation on the pyramid. Many well-known explorers made a point of visiting the pyramid. Down through the ages countless other people have visited the Great Pyramid, while many others have never been there but have undertaken a lifelong study of it. People from different cultures, time periods, rich and poor, have been drawn to the Great Pyramid. What are they searching for?

Could it be that people are drawn to the Great Pyramid of Giza because they are searching for answers about life and unconsciously feel that the answers lie there? Maybe they want to know who they are, where they have come from, the nature of the afterlife, the nature of God, and they think the pyramid may help them in their search. Since the Great Pyramid has always been shrouded in mystery, maybe they think it holds the answers to some of these questions.

Throughout history, mountains, monuments, and other elevated places, have often been associated with God and His revelations to man.

Moses received the Ten Commandments from God on Mount Sinai. Hammurabi, King of the Babylonian Empire, received the Code of Hammurabi, which became one of the first written legal codes in history, from God on a mountain. The Tower of Babel was built to reach heaven. Legend has it that there was a mountain in the

center of Atlantis that reached up to heaven. We build cathedrals and churches to symbolize reaching up to heaven. The Great Pyramid was the highest structure in ancient times and was perhaps another stepping stone to God.

IN THE KING'S CHAMBER

Many people who have spent time in the King's Chamber alone have reported paranormal and psychic experiences. Some of them claim out-of-body experiences, others hear noises and see visions. One interesting book mentioned by many researchers is *A Search in Secret Egypt* by Paul Brunton, published in 1936. He describes a fascinating out-of-body experience during the night he spent alone in the King's Chamber. He claims to have seen demons and the spirit of an Egyptian high priest. This priest caused him to leave his body and explore the pyramid and its secret passageways in his astral body. He was shown secrets before eventually finding himself back in his physical body. This might be easily dismissed as fantasy, but reports of this type of paranormal event as experienced by many credible researchers are quite frequent.

RADIOACTIVITY & GRANITE

Recent studies have shown that locations with high levels of radioactivity tend to produce altered states and paranormal phenomena in individuals who stay in those areas for a period of time. Many ancient monuments are associated with this high level of radioactivity. Is it possible that the radioactivity affects the brain and causes a distortion in perception? Alternatively, could it be opening a gateway to another dimension or world? Perhaps there is a radioactive receptor in our brain responsible for these phenomena in such locations.

The Great Pyramid is mostly built of limestone, but the King's Chamber is constructed of granite. Paul Devereux, author of the book *Places of Power*

(1996), as well as others, has said that granite was a spirit stone to the ancient Egyptians. The walls, ceiling, and floor of the King's Chamber are composed of one hundred blocks of granite. The relieving chambers above are also composed of granite. Thus, only this area of the pyramid is composed of granite, and this is the exact location where paranormal phenomena have been experienced. Devereux measured levels of radioactivity in the King's Chamber and found there to be a significantly higher count than in the surrounding desert.

Devereux points out that some of the ancient megalithic structures also have high levels of radioactivity that range between two to three times higher than their environment. In fact, he found anomalies in high radiation levels from over a dozen sites in Britain. Were these structures built in specific areas because there was already a high level of radioactivity there? Or were these sites chosen because a number of paranormal phenomena had already been observed there? Devereux's work may shed some light on scientifically understanding paranormal phenomena.

ABOVE
Recent studies have found that the sites of ancient monuments, such as the one above, are often associated with high levels of radioactivity and paranormal phenomena.

LEFT
Many people consider the King's Chamber in the Great Pyramid to be the most sacred place on earth. Many visitors have chosen to lie and meditate in its empty Coffer. Some people claim to have had psychic experiences, especially if left alone here.

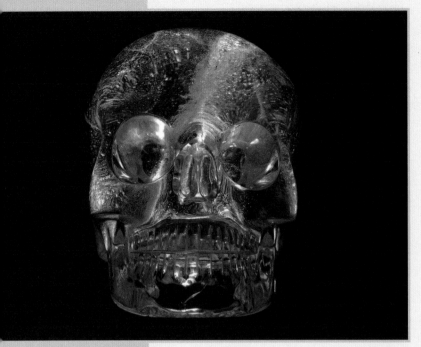

ABOVE

A crystal skull, displayed in the British Museum. Crystal skulls are one of the most mysterious artifacts on the planet. Ancient cultures did not have the technology to produce them. The purpose and production of crystal skulls remain a mystery. The skull in this photograph is alleged to be from the ancient Aztec civilization.

RIGHT

Recent remote sensing has detected an enormous underground complex underneath the Giza Plateau. Is it possible that this ancient structure connects the entire Giza complex? Could this help answer some of our questions about the pyramids?

CRYSTAL SKULLS

F.R."Nick" Nocerino was a gifted psychic involved in teaching and researching metaphysical phenomena for most of his life. He was one of the first people in the U.S.A. in the 1950s to use and study crystals. He was also one of the first Ghost Hunters, and used to appear frequently on television and radio shows discussing his work Nocerino was involved in pyramid research for many years and repeated many of the experiments of Antoine Bovis and Karl Drbal (see Chapter 15).

Nocerino was one of the few people to own an ancient crystal skull. In the 1950s, while he was excavating in Mexico, he found a human-sized crystal skull in the buried ruins of an ancient city. The tomb in which it was found was dated at over 2,000 years old. The most famous of all the ancient crystal skulls is the one that the explorer F.A. Mitchell-Hedges and his adopted daughter, Anna, claimed to have discovered in 1924 in ancient Mayan ruins in Lubaantun, Belize. It is carved from a single block of quartz rock crystal and polished

into the shape of a life-sized human skull. Many experts who examined this skull suggested it may be at least 3,000 years old. Others dispute this claim. Hewlett-Packard scientists examined it in the 1960s and concluded that it would have taken 300 years to make this skull. This is mainly due to the ancient techniques that would have been employed, i.e. polishing the skull either by hand or by using whatever was available in nature at the time. However, the skull should not exist because the culture at that time would not have had the technology to manufacture it. The purpose of the skull remains a mystery, but paranormal activity seems to occur in its vicinity.

UNDERGROUND & AT THE SUMMIT

During one of our conversations in which we were discussing the ancient Egyptians and their use of crystals, Nocerino told me about a fascinating

LEFT
Members of the Adventurers'
Club of Denmark on the
summit of the Great Pyramid
in 1963. Notice that there
is room on top to be able to
walk around freely. Many
believe that the summit of
the Great Pyramid is the most
sacred part of it. High levels
of electromagnetic energy
have also been recorded
at the summit.

experience that he had on his first visit to the Great Pyramid of Giza during World War II. He was a first class seaman in the U.S. Navy and was assigned to operate the machine gun on a truck carrying supplies and servicemen to Morocco, Algeria, and Egypt. During a three-day pass, he visited the Great Pyramid with two of his friends. As he explored the different passageways and chambers, he felt a presence the entire time. He also felt an increasing energy force pushing on him, which made him want to leave. When he went back to the passageway leading to the outside of the pyramid, he had the feeling of hands holding him back.

As for the creators of the pyramids, Nocerino believed that some kind of society or group lived on Earth in very ancient times but was wiped out, or had to leave, for some reason, possibly because of a catastrophe that changed its environment. Nick believed that this culture left its records either in a secret chamber in the Great Pyramid, or more likely in a hidden chamber underneath it, or in other structures around Egypt. Recently, remote sensing has detected an incredibly large underground complex beneath the Giza Plateau with networks of tunnels. As yet we do not know when or why they were constructed. One possibility is that the entire Giza complex is connected by this very ancient underground structure. When it is finally explored, something may be discovered that will shed some light on the mysteries of the pyramids.

Nick thought that the most sacred site in the Great Pyramid was the summit. He emphasized that the summit was a very special energy center. Remember also that Joe Parr (see Chapter 14) recorded high levels of electromagnetic energy at the summit of the Great Pyramid.

Nick also said that he would never spend a night in the Great Pyramid because anyone sensitive to the forces that pervade it would not want to be left there alone.

Texts were first written thousands or even tens of thousands of years ago, long before the dynastic period ever began in Egypt. The purpose of this manual could have been lost to later civilizations, like the ancient Egyptians. Maybe the civilization that used it disappeared, and when the manual was rediscovered by the ancient Egyptians, they had no idea as to its real purpose. Maybe they assumed it to be some kind of religious text, and decided to change and edit it over the years to fit their beliefs. Thus, what we have today is some form of corrupted manual. The question is: What kind of manual was it originally?

As one starts to analyze the Pyramid Texts individually and look at specifics, it appears that they are describing some kind of space travel. After all, the ancient Egyptian religion is based on the symbolism of the stars, and there are many examples of this in other ancient Egyptian writings, for example, the later texts written on coffins and in the *Book of the Dead*. Was some ancient civilization actually capable of travelling into space, and did they have a corresponding descriptive manual? Is the ancient Egyptian religion based upon this manual for space travel, the true purpose of which was lost to them?

THE PYRAMID TEXTS

Some of the oldest known religious writings in the world come from Egypt and are known as the "Pyramid Texts." They consist of approximately 200 hieroglyphic spells which have been found written mostly on Egyptian Middle Kingdom coffins. These hieroglyphics are also found inscribed on the walls of certain pyramids. The Pharaoh Unis, who ruled Egypt between 2356-2323 BCE had his pyramid (which is not very large) built at Saqqara. The hieroglyphics covering the inside walls are the oldest inscriptions found in Egypt. Several translations are available, the best in my opinion being by Raymond O. Faulkner (1894–1982), a British Egyptologist and philologist of the ancient Egyptian language.

During one of my readings of the Pyramid Texts something struck me. I got the distinct impression that these texts were originally written to be a manual, and must have been corrupted or changed later. As a scientist and former college professor, I am used to reading all kinds of scientific manuals. Maybe the Pyramid

The Great Pyramid plays a very important symbolic role in the ancient Egyptian religion. We have also noted that the orientation of the pyramid and the airshafts in the main chambers point to specific constellations and stars such as Orion. The Egyptians believed that when the Pharaoh died, he traveled to the constellation Orion and became a star. This was where one entered the afterlife, the dwelling place of the soul.

ANCIENT & MODERN

Another interesting observation is that of the similarity between mummies and the spacesuits of astronauts. Maybe mummification is the corrupted process of how space travelers would prepare their bodies for interstellar travel. Joe Parr, whose research is discussed in Chapter 14, identified a neutrino conduit from the sun to Orion. Every time the Earth passes through this conduit, strange things happen in or with his model pyramids. Was this the conduit that was used for space travel? Did the interstellar traveler prepare himself in such a way that he would resemble a mummy?

Another theory is that this manual may have been used for travel between worlds in different dimensions, or to the world of the dead, or to alternate states of consciousness. The Egyptians were fascinated with the world of the dead. Could these journeys have been something like out-of-body experiences and thus, the travelers would need their bodies to remain alive and intact in order to return to them? This may have led to the religious belief in preserving the bodies of mummies for eternity. Admittedly, this speculation stretches credulity and would make good reading in a science-fiction novel. But remember that most of what ancient peoples observed was considered miraculous or magical until scientific laws were eventually discovered. There may be higher laws of physics waiting to be discovered, ones that transcend our understanding.

There are also certain types of electromagnetic energy that humans cannot directly feel, but other animals can. Bees can see in the ultraviolet spectrum and rattlesnakes in the infrared spectrum. So is the energy behind paranormal phenomena an undiscovered type that some can perceive while others are unable to? While it is tempting to speculate, we must remember as scientists to always seek facts and proof. For now these ideas remain speculation only, but who knows what may be revealed in the future.

DECODING

In this book, we have explored many diverse theories about the Great Pyramid of Giza. Yet fundamentally we still do not know for sure who built it, nor when, how, and why it was built.

One of the purposes of the Great Pyramid of Giza Research Association is to deal with the larger mystery and the essential unknowns at work in the Great Pyramid. Our researchers, from many diverse disciplines, work independently, but also come together to try to answer these enigmatic questions. Maybe one day we will have the answers to some or all of these questions, but for now we do not know and are still searching. Maybe you will play a role. If you would like to contact the Association, please visit our website at www.gizapyramid.com and email us.

PART FOUR

THE APPENDICES

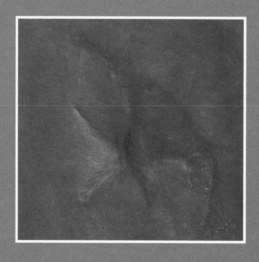

"It seems that the building of pyramids
is something deeply rooted in our
human consciousness."

HISTORICAL ACCOUNTS

Throughout history, many have been hypnotized by the beauty and mystery of the Great Pyramid. Some have even dedicated their lives to studying it. This section provides information about many of the early visitors to the Great Pyramid. Some of what they found, thought, did, and wrote is recorded here.

BREYDENBACK 1484

He published his book, *Breydenback's Travels*, in 1486 after visiting the Great Pyramid. He thought that it was built by the biblical Joseph for storing grain for seven years of the coming famine.

MARTINI Á BAUMGARTEN 1507

A German, he wrote: "For the magnificence and art that is displayed upon them, they may justly be reckoned one of the Seven Wonders of the World … the greatest of these … is so large still, that the strongest man that is, standing and throwing a dart straight forwards, can scarcely reach the middle of it; which experiment has been oftentimes tried."

PIERRE BELON 1546

A Frenchman, he reported seeing inside the Great Pyramid, "a vast tomb of black marble." He was most likely referring to the Coffer.

JEAN CHESNEAU 1546

Secretary to the French Ambassador, he climbed to the top of the Great Pyramid. He reported that: "Near it [the Great Pyramid] are two others, not so large, and not thus made in degrees [steps] and they are without openings." From this account it appears that at this date the Great Pyramid was the only one of the three stripped of its casing stones.

ANDRÉ THEVET CHAPLIAN 1549

Cartographer to the king of France, he reported seeing "a great stone of marble carved in the manner of a sepulcher." He was obviously referring to the Coffer in the King's Chamber.

JOHANNES HELFERICH 1565

He reported that the courses of the stones were very high, and that the pyramid was accessible only on one of the corner angles. He also said that

there was a very welcome resting place halfway up. It is interesting that almost everyone who has climbed to the top mentions this resting place or chasm. This is probably a spot on the northeast side of the Great Pyramid produced either through natural erosion or man-made by early explorers.

JEAN PALERME 1581

The brother of Henry III of France, he wrote: "The Great Pyramid surpasses the others in magnificence and is superior to the antiquities of ancient Rome." He climbed to the summit and claimed to have a caught a white bird on the top (known as a Pharaoh's hen). He also mentions the numerous bats in the Grand Gallery, and observed that the Coffer had no lid and that it was composed of the same stone (red granite) as the walls, and it sounded like a bell when struck. He took a piece away with him and this may be partially the cause of the damage at the corner of the Coffer.

LAURENCE ALDERSEY 1586

After visiting the pyramid, he said that, "The monuments bee high and in forme four-square and every one of the squares as long as a man may shoote a roving arrowe, and as high as a church."

PROPER ALPIN 1591

A physician from Venice, he stated that the Well Shaft in the subterranean chamber did not contain any water, even though he went down for a distance of 70 ft (21 m). Of the Coffer in the King's Chamber he observed: "Upon being struck, it sounded like a bell."

FRANÇOIS SAVARY DE BRÈVES 1605

He was the French ambassador. On entering the King's Chamber, he remarked that "the joints between the huge stones are so marvelously trimmed that one could not insert the point of a needle without difficulty."

GEORGE SANDYS 1610

A noted traveler and author of *Sandy's Travells*, he wrote: "The name [Pyramid] is derived from a flame of fire, in regard to their shape; broad below, and sharp above, like a pointed diamond. By such the ancients did express the original of things; and that formless form-making substance. For as a Pyramid beginning at a point, and the principal height by little and little dilateth into all parts; so Nature proceeding from one undividable fountain (even God the Sovereign Essence), receiveth diversity of forms; effused into several kinds and multitudes of figures; uniting all in the Supreme Head, from whence all excellencies issue."

After climbing to the top, Sandys recorded that, "During a great part of the day, it casteth no shadow on the earth, but is at once illuminated on all sides." This would happen when the sun is very high in the sky and directly above the pyramid.

PIETRO DELLA VALLE 1616

An Italian, he remarked that the sarcophagus in the King's Chamber was made of so hard a stone that he tried in vain to break it with a hatchet and that it sounded like a bell and had not any cover. He also observed some Turks shoot several arrows from the top of the pyramid, but none reached the ground beyond the base.

M. DE VILLAMONT 1618

After climbing to the top of the Great Pyramid he reported that his guide, "could not shoot an arrow beyond the base." While there, he was told an interesting story. It seemed that a man who had been condemned to death was given the opportunity by the Pasha in Cairo to be let down into the Well Shaft to look for treasure. Towards the bottom, the rope broke and his light went out. He eventually found his way out, and the next day he made his way up the Descending Passage and received the Pasha's pardon.

JOHN GREAVES *FIRST VISIT 1638*

The author of the first scientific work on the pyramids, Greaves was Professor of Astronomy at Oxford. He believed that the Great Pyramid was built during the reign of Khufu as a tomb for the Pharaoh.

M. DE MONCONYS *1647*

A French traveler, he observed that the Well Shaft was deep and had no other opening than the top. He believed it was meant to connect to the Sphinx.

M. TREVENOT *1655*

He reported the experience of a Scotsman who was lowered down the Well Shaft. He wrote: "The Well was not entirely perpendicular; it went down about sixty-seven feet [20.4 m] to a grotto, from whence it again descended to a depth of one hundred and twenty-three feet [37.4 m], when it was filled up with sand. It contained an immense quantity of bats, so that the Scotsman was afraid of being eaten up by them, and was obliged to guard the candle with his hands."

MELTON *1661*

A British traveler, he visited the pyramids and and reported that the Arabs called them "The Mountains of Pharaoh." He climbed to the summit of the Great Pyramid and also explored the interior. He attempted to break off a piece of the Coffer, using a hammer he'd brought for that purpose. The stone was so hard that he was not able to break off even a small piece. He noted, however, that when struck, it gave "a sound like a bell which could be heard at a great distance."

VAUSLEB *1664*

He remarked that the Grand Gallery was lofty and well-built. He observed an aperture in a wall in the King's Chamber (the Southern Airshaft) and said he could not understand what its purpose was.

ATHANASIUS KIRCHER *1666*

He believed that obelisks and pyramids have mystical and hidden significance. He was the first, as far as we know, to propose this view of the hidden or symbolic significance of the Great Pyramid.

BENOIT DE MAILLET *1692-1708*

Consul General in Egypt from 1692–1708, he was one of the first to make a serious study of the Great Pyramid. He believed that the Pharaoh was interred in the King's Chamber, the passages were then sealed up, and the workmen left via the Well Shaft.

GEMELLI CARERI *1693*

After visiting the Great Pyramid, he was one of the first to suggest that, in addition to being a tomb, it was used for astronomical purposes. Others after him have speculated about this too. It is possible that before the pyramid was completed, when the Grand Gallery was open to the sky, it could have served as an astronomical observatory. Again, this is speculation, but also a possibility.

PAUL LUCAS *1699*

He traveled to the pyramids as a treasure hunter: "to collect gems, coins, and curios for sale." As far as we know, he found nothing.

ELLIS VERYARD *1701*

A medical doctor from London, he climbed the Great Pyramid and describes his adventure thus: "The exterior was in the form of steps, by which we ascended, but not without some difficulty and danger, from the irregularity and decayed state of the stones. At about half of the ascent, we found a place, which seemed expressly made for a resting place for travelers, capable of holding nine or ten persons. After remaining here for some time, we proceeded to the top; which, although when viewed from below, it appears to end in a point, can

nevertheless contain forty persons with great ease. From thence, we had a prospect on one side of the barren sandy deserts of Africa; and on the other, of Cairo, the Nile, and the adjoining country, with all the towers and villages."

PAUL LUCAS *1714*

He proposed that the pyramid was a giant sundial and would indicate the solstices. This is an interesting idea since the pyramid does cast shadows and could act as a sundial.

ABOVE
Painting of Osiris, one of
the oldest gods of Ancient
Egypt. A visitor to the Great
Pyramid in 1721 believed
that its interior passages and
chambers were created for
the mystical worship of Osiris.

were ramps on each side and quadrangular holes over them and it was constructed with slabs of marble (limestone) so finely put together that the joints could scarcely be perceived and the walls became gradually narrower towards the top by the overlapping of the courses of masonry." He also remarked that the Coffer gave off a sonorous sound and did not have any inscription on it.

CARSTON NIEBUHR 1761

He observed that the Great Pyramid was oriented to the four cardinal directions (north-south-east-west). Many megalithic sites are oriented to specific directions, such as to the north or the east, where the sun rises.

NATHANIEL DAVISON 1763–65

The British Consul at Algiers, he explored the Great Pyramid and was the first to discover the first relieving chamber above the King's Chamber, which was later named "Davison's Chamber."

THOMAS SHAW 1721

Shaw observed that the core masonry contained fossil shells, and was one of the first to record that the blocks are composed of nummulitic limestone (a rock formed chiefly by the accumulation of fossils). He believed that interior passages and chambers were intended for the mystical worship of Osiris. Thus the Great Pyramid was essentially a temple used for initiation into the mysteries.

DR. PERRY 1743

His visit to the Great Pyramid led him to the conclusion that it was built as a place for religious rites and mysteries.

ABBÉ CLAUDE-LOUIS FOURMONT 1753

In his account of his visit to the Great Pyramid, he described the Grand Gallery as "very magnificent both in workmanship and materials …There

NAPOLEON BONAPARTE 1798

The French invaded Egypt in 1798 under Napoleon Bonaparte and there was a large battle at Embaba, located about 10 miles (16 km) from the Great Pyramid. Historians refer to this as "The Battle of the Pyramids." Addressing his troops before the big battle, Napoleon said, "Soldiers, from the height of these pyramids forty centuries are watching us."

While sitting at the base of the pyramid, Napoleon calculated that there was enough stone in all three of the Giza pyramids to build a 10 ft (3 m) high, 1 ft (0.3 m) thick wall around France. He also took with him a group of 175 civilians, known as "savants," who were archeologists, engineers, surveyors, artists, scholars, etcetera, and they remained in Egypt until 1801. They studied and surveyed the pyramids and archeological monuments in detail and recorded their research.

Eventually, large volumes were published about their research in Egypt from 1809 to 1822 by order of the then emperor, Napoleon Bonaparte. One of the main "savants," Edmé-Francois Jomard wrote, "Above all, in the First [Great] Pyramid the funereal purpose is far from being the primary object and it has not even been proved that any king was ever placed therein after his death." Dominique Vivant Denon also said that neither Khufu nor Chephren were actually interred in their pyramids.

It should be mentioned that the Rosetta Stone was discovered in 1799 by an officer of the Engineers of the French Military. The Rosetta stone is a large black stone stele, or slab, with writing on it in three languages. It was discovered in the city of Rosetta, a harbor on the Mediterranean coast of Egypt. The three languages inscribed on it were hieroglyphics, Egyptian Demotic, and Classical Greek. This stone became the basis for the decipherment of hieroglyphics. It is believed to have been created around 200 BCE.

GIOVANNI BATTISTA CAVIGLIA 1817

An Italian seaman, he cleared the Well Shaft of the Great Pyramid. He demonstrated that the end of the Well Shaft ended in the subterranean section of the Descending Passage.

ABOVE
A scene from the Battle of the Pyramids during the French invasion of Egypt in 1798. From the base of the Great Pyramid, Napoleon calculated that there was enough stone in the three pyramids of Giza to build a wall around France 10 ft (3 m) high and 1 ft (0.3 m) thick.

LEFT
The Rosetta Stone. This large stone stele was discovered in 1799. The writing on the stone, in three different languages, was used for deciphering hieroglyphics.

THOMAS YEATES *1833*

An English biblical scholar, he wrote in 1833, "The Great Pyramid soon followed the Tower of Babel, and had the same common origin. Whether it was not a copy of the original Tower of Babel? And, moreover, whether the dimensions of these structures were not originally taken from the Ark of Noah? The measures of the Great Pyramid at the base do so approximate to the measures of the Ark of Noah in ancient cubit measure, that I cannot scruple, however novel the idea, to draw a comparison."

COLONEL HOWARD VYSE *1837*

Vyse used drastic means to explore the pyramids and this can be seen today in the large gash on the southern face of the Great Pyramid, which was caused by blasting with gunpowder. He is most famous for his three-volume work, *Operations Carried on at the Pyramids of Gizeh in 1837.* Unfortunately, these volumes are very rare and very expensive to come by. Colonel Vyse also worked with the civil engineer, John Perring. Perring wrote a two-volume work, *The Pyramids of Gizeh*, published in 1839-40. Together they discovered the remaining four upper relieving chambers above the King's Chamber.

MR. WATHEN *1842*

After visiting the pyramids he remarked that, "The offerings of the Queen of Sheba are now beheld in the indestructible masses of the pyramids." Thus they were the Queen of Sheba's gifts.

M. FIALIN DE PERSIGNY *1845*

He expressed the opinion that the purpose of the pyramids was to act a a barrier against the sandy eruptions of the desert in Egypt and Nubia.

FLINDERS PETRIE *1881*

Petrie accomplished a complete survey of the pyramids, measuring all 203 courses. His work was published in 1883 in a book called *The Pyramids and Temples of Gizeh.*

BELOW

Painting of the Tower of Babel. It has been suggested that the Great Pyramid has the same common origin as the Tower of Babel, and could possibly be a copy of the original tower.

JOHN AND MORTON EDGAR 1891

These brothers explored the Great Pyramid and published excellent black and white photographs in their two-volume work, *Great Pyramid Passages*. The Edgar brothers also supported the idea of pyramidology and that the pyramid was of divine inspiration.

GEORGE REISNER 1939

An American Egyptologist, he made the first radio broadcast from inside the King's Chamber.

Here are some other novel ideas from individuals around the mid 1800s.

A Swedish philosopher thought the pyramids were structures for purifying the water of the muddy Nile, which passed through their passages.

A Mr. Gable said that, "It appears not that the founders of them had any such laudable design of transmitting to posterity specimens, as some had supposed; hence they appear to have been erected for no geometrical purpose. They were erected by those who, after their intermarriages with the daughters of men, became not only degenerate despisers of useful knowledge but altogether abandoned to luxury." Thus, he felt the pyramids were built to please these women, who had requested that the sons of God employ their leisure in that manner.

The Reverend E.B. Zincke had a more practical suggestion. "In those days, labor could not be bottled up. Egypt was so fertile, and men's wants were then so few, that surplus labor was available, and much food, from taxes in kind, accumulated in royal hands." So, the pyramid was built to employ workers who had no jobs and to use up the excess money in the treasury.

BELOW

The desert plateau of Giza, adjacent to the pyramids. Were the pyramids built as barriers against the encroaching desert sands of Egypt and the Sudan?

MODEL PYRAMIDS

I would like to thank my very good friend and research colleague Dr. Patrick Flanagan for permission to reprint some of the material and diagrams from his book Pyramid Power, *published in 1973, which was the first best-selling book written about pyramids.*

O ne of the most frequent questions I am asked by many people, including students, is how to build a small model pyramid and perform experiments with it. In his book, Dr. Flanagan gives specific directions, which I will summarize below. These pyramids can be used for student science projects and are fairly easy to make. We cannot guarantee the results, but if you follow the directions carefully then your chances of a successful experiment will increase.

Since the publication of Dr. Flanagan's book, countless numbers of people have experimented with model pyramids. Many have obtained interesting results and contributed to the literature of pyramid research. The most important considerations are that both the dimensions and orientation of the model pyramid be correct.

Dr. Flanagan's main interest lay in the effect that pyramids have on living organisms such as plants and people. He used various scientific devices to measure the changes. He and others have tried these experiments with differently-shaped objects (cubes, octagons, hexagons, etcetera) but have not achieved the same results. The pyramid shape is truly unique.

To begin, we first need to build our model pyramid. It can be built from cardboard, wood, Plexiglas, steel, copper, aluminum, or various other materials. It seems that the type of material does not matter as long as the size and orientation of the pyramid are correct.

In his book, Dr. Flanagan provided a chart with dimensions for building pyramids of different heights. The chart includes pyramids that range from 3.8 to 45.8 in (9.65 to 116.33 cm) high.

These dimensions are based on those of the Great Pyramid of Giza. Dr. Flanagan also experimented with pyramids that had windows or holes in their sides. Since the Great Pyramid is ventilated (by the airshafts in the King's Chamber), he thought these would facilitate the results, which it seemed to do. If you would like to

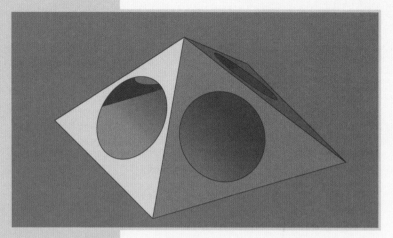

ABOVE

Dr. Flanagan experimented with pyramids with holes or windows in their sides. These are based on the airshafts that ventilate the Great Pyramid. The holes should be up to a third of the base length of the pyramid in diameter.

PREVIOUS PAGE

View of the Great Pyramid illuminated at night.

add windows or holes, they should be up to a third of the base length of the pyramid in diameter. The illustration above shows an example.

Dr. Flanagan believes that a pyramid's best alignment is with one of the sides facing magnetic north, so you would need a good compass to indicate where magnetic north is.

One of the easiest experiments to perform is to build a model pyramid the size of your choice out of heavy cardboard, using the chart below. Ensure the holes you make in the pyramid are as specified above. Make two identical pyramids. One will be your "control group." Make sure that you do not place the two pyramids too close together. Keep them at least several feet apart in a similar environment so you can minimize other

Dimensions for Model Pyramid

Base	Side	Height (approx.)
6 in (15.24 cm)	5.7 in (14.47 cm)	3.8 in (9.65 cm)
12 in (30.48 cm)	11.4 in (28.95 cm)	7.6 in (19.3 cm)
24 in (60.96 cm)	22.8 in (57.91 cm)	15.3 in (38.86 cm)
36 in (91.44 cm)	34.3 in (87.12 cm)	22.9 in (58.16 cm)
72 in (182.88 cm)	68.5 in (173.99 cm)	45.8 in (116.33 cm)

variables. Place a platform in the center of each of the pyramids that extends about a third of the way up. It seems that the strongest energy field generated in a pyramid is about a third up from the base in the middle of the pyramid. This base could also be made out of cardboard.

Place some food such as cheese, meat, or fruit on the platform of both pyramids. Now here is the difference. Using a compass, align *one* of the sides of one of the pyramids to magnetic north. Align the other pyramid differently, maybe just randomly, but make sure none of the sides are pointing to magnetic north. You can also just put a piece of the food on a platform with no pyramid above it. The idea is to be able to compare the results of food preservation in a pyramid aligned to magnetic north versus food decomposing naturally outside a pyramid. Many people have reported that the pyramid helps preserve food.

You can try the food experiment for different lengths of time, for several days if not longer. Obviously, this will depend on the type of food you use. Meat, for example, will go bad more quickly than cheese, which will show greater results sooner. If you are performing this experiment for a science fair, I suggest you take a photograph of the food (including the control group) every day to show the changes.

This experiment will not always work, but your chances of success are better if you follow all of the directions.

Dr. Flanagan performed an unusual experiment with these model pyramids. He used a technique known as Kirlian photography to evaluate the effect of pyramids on plants and humans. Kirlian photography is named after its inventor, Semyon Kirlian, who in 1939 discovered that if an object is placed on a photographic plate and connected to a high-voltage source, an electrical discharge, or corona, is produced on the film. Many people believed that this was a photograph of the aura

of living things. Many now believe it can register the supernatural aura of the body, for example, acupuncture points correspond to this aura. Dr. Flanagan measured the Kirlian aura of a human finger before and after treatment in a model pyramid. The subject was placed in a simple 6-ft (1.82-m) base vinyl plastic pyramid properly aligned to the magnetic poles, and was in the pyramid for varying times. The results show that the band of energy, or aura, around the finger was rounder and larger when it was in the pyramid compared with outside the pyramid.

A more dramatic effect was obtained from a geranium leaf. The leaf was removed from its plant for thirty minutes before the first Kirlian photograph was taken. In the image opposite, you can see that the energy field has almost dissipated indicating that the leaf was dying. This same leaf was then placed in a 6-in (15.2-cm) base pyramid made of cardboard and properly aligned for five minutes. You can see that the aura has increased considerably showing that the leaf has recovered.

Finally, it is interesting to show an illustration of one of Dr. Flanagan's inventions. It is a small aluminium plate, $\frac{1}{8}$ in (0.063 cm) thick, with a matrix of fifteen pyramids which he electronically charged with "amplified" pyramid energy. He has shown that this structure does actually produce energy fields from the tops of the pyramids.

APPENDIX THREE

PYRAMIDS ON MARS

So far, we have discussed not only the Great Pyramid of Giza but also the Russian pyramids and those found in other parts of the world. It seems that the building of pyramids is something that is deeply rooted in human consciousness and transcends all cultures and time.

C ould this motivation to build pyramids be a universal phenomenon and could there be pyramids on other planets in our solar system?

One of the most incredible technological accomplishments that man has achieved has been to send space probes to Mars to photograph and study its surface. Mariner 9, a NASA spacecraft launched on May 30, 1971, reached the orbit of Mars the same year on November 14. It orbited Mars for 349 days and took 7,329 images. These photographs covered about 80 percent of the surface of Mars and showed craters, possibly dried river beds, extinct volcanoes, canyons, and other surface features. Images were also taken of the two tiny moons of Mars, Phobos and Deimos.

THE ELYSIUM QUADRANGLE

What was unusual was that at a latitude of 15 degrees north and a longitude of 198 degrees west, a Mariner image revealed what looked like

a group of tetrahedral (three-sided) pyramids. (Remember that the Great Pyramid and most other pyramids on Earth are four-sided.) They were located on a barren plateau known as the Elysium Quadrangle.

Dr. J.J. Hurtak, one of the research directors of our Association and a specialist in remote sensing, was one of the first scientists to identify and study these structures. Comparisons between two separate photographs (two different fly-bys of that area) taken at different sun angles confirmed that these structures were precise pyramidal formations and not shadowy patterns or artifacts caused by the film.

Dr. Hurtak believes that these structures "are far too unique to be simply written off as natural phenomena." He published his findings in 1974 and was one of the first to make this information available to a wider audience. (As we saw in Chapter 9, Hurtak was also the researcher who, in 1973, first advanced

ABOVE & BELOW
NASA images of the Elysium pyramids taken by Mariner 9. Comparisons of two different photographs show that these structures are precise pyramidal formations.

the alignment between the Southern Airshaft in the King's Chamber of the Great Pyramid and the three stars in the belt of Orion.) Image enhancement of these pyramids on Mars revealed that the larger pyramids may be over 3,000 ft (914 m) high and the smaller ones about 1,500 ft (457 m) high. This would be over six times the height and seven hundred times the volume of the Great Pyramid of Giza.

The famous astronomer and author Carl Sagan also mentions these Elysium pyramids in his book *Cosmos*, published in 1980. It has been suggested that possible causes of these pyramid shapes could be high wind storms, erosion, glacial sculpturing, and other natural phenomena. NASA performed tests to simulate these conditions, using wind tunnels and other equipment, but could not adequately reproduce the effect. So the debate continues as to whether these pyramids are natural or not.

Since the 1970s, this has been a hotly debated subject. Some believe the evidence to be overwhelming that these pyramids are not natural phenomena, but man-made, or rather "Martian-made." Were there once, in the distant past, living beings with intelligence on Mars who were part of a civilization that may have built these pyramids? Did this civilization die out and are these pyramids the remnants of their culture?

CYDONIA

The Elysium Quadrangle is not the only area on Mars where pyramids have been discovered. Pyramid structures have also been identified in the area known as Cydonia. It lies at a latitude of 41 degrees north and a longitude of 351 degrees east. In 1976 the Viking Mars probe photographed this area, as did the Global Surveyor in 1998.

This area was again photographed at a much higher resolution in 2001. Besides the pyramid structures, this is the area where the alleged 1,500 ft (457 m) high Face on Mars was discovered, which resembles the Sphinx in Egypt. In the photograph to the right, you can see that at a higher resolution this "face" proves to be a natural formation. The face effect was produced by lights and shadows. Thus, there really is no "face" on Mars.

The pyramids in this region of Cydonia are another story. There are what appear to be one five-sided pyramid and over twelve tetrahedral pyramids. Again, the question remains as to whether these structures are natural or made by some intelligent beings. Unless astronauts can land at that site or we obtain much higher resolution photographs, this will remain an ongoing debate.

MARS & EGYPT

How does Mars relate to Egypt? According to Dr. Hurtak, who has a background in linguistics, one of the interesting facts about the Great Pyramid is that it was built near the city of Cairo which, by its very name, is linked to Mars. The name given to the area of Cairo by Arab scholars is "Al Qahirah." This is an epithet signifying the "Victorious One" or the "Conqueror." However, the same Arabic name in its masculine form, "Al Qahir," is given to the planet Mars.

The foundation stone for the city of Cairo was laid under the direction of Mohammed's daughter, Fatima, in the 7th century CE. According to legend, Mars was in unique alignment with the city site at that time. Arab astronomers considered this a special sign from Allah and thus suggested the original name for the city as "Al Qahir" (the city of the Victorious One). Since all cities were considered by the Arabs to be feminine in gender, this was later feminized to "Al Qahirah." The linguistic root for "Al Qahir" was, incidentally, originally "to be bright, to be illustrious." Thus, the Ancients entertained a special planetary connection between Cairo (including the area of Giza) and the planet Mars.

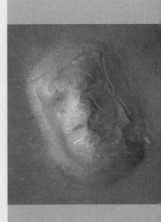

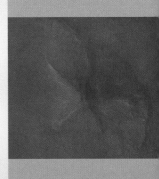

PYRAMIDS OF THE WORLD

One question that arises quite frequently is how the Great Pyramid of Giza differs from other pyramids around the world. Large pyramids have been found in Mexico and Central America, South America, the Middle East, and the Far East, including some underwater pyramids in Japan. Pyramids have also been found all over Europe.

OTHER EGYPTIAN PYRAMIDS

The "great age of pyramid building" in ancient Egypt, which occurred during the Old Kingdom, witnessed the steady refinement of architectural techniques, culminating in the construction of the Great Pyramid. Two of the most well-known pyramids that contributed to this outstanding technical development are the Step Pyramid at Saqqara and the Bent Pyramid at Dahshur.

RIGHT

The Step Pyramid was built in the reign of the Pharaoh Djoser, *c.* 2630–2611 BCE. At approximately 200 ft (60 m) high, the pyramid was designed by the royal architect, Imhotep.

BELOW

The original sides of the Bent Pyramid were extremely steep at 54 degrees. It became clear that the resulting structure would not be stable. Thus the incline was reduced for the higher stages to 43 degrees.

THE NUBIAN PYRAMIDS
IN SUDAN

A total of 223 pyramids were built in ancient Nubia by the Kushites. The largest site is at Meroe, which lies about 125 miles (200 km) north-east of Khartoum, Sudan. This royal cemetery is all that remains of the Meroitic kingdom (c. 300 BCE to 300 CE). The pyramids here represent a continuation of the pharonic burial practice that had died out in Egypt hundreds of years before.

LEFT AND BELOW
These beautiful and ancient structures at Meroe have suffered severe damage from the elements, especially as after they were excavated in the 19th century, they were left unprotected during the 20th century. Today, preservation work is underway, funded and supported by the Sudanese government with the help of international aid.

MESO-AMERICAN PYRAMIDS

Apart from the Egyptian pyramids, the most well-known ones are those found in Mexico and Central America. One important difference is that, while the purpose of the Great Pyramid remains something of a mystery, archeologists believe that the Meso-American pyramids were used for ritual and astronomical purposes.

RIGHT

The Pyramid of the Sun at Teotihuacán, Mexico, is the third largest pyramid in the world. It was constructed by the Teotihuacano people in two phases, beginning around 100 CE. However, it was the Aztecs, who visited the city centuries after it was abandoned, who gave the pyramid its name..

RIGHT

Monte Alban, in Oaxaca, Mexico, was a holy city built by the Zapotecs. It reached its zenith *c.* 300 CE. The pyramid complex, known as "System IV," lies on the west side of this extensive site, and would once have been topped with a wooden temple.

LEFT

The Pyramid of the Niches at El Tajín, Mexico, is an intricate step pyramid some 60 ft (18 m) high. There are 365 niches cut into the terraces, and a staircase running up the east side.

BELOW

The Mayan site at Edzná contains this remarkable temple, built in pyramid-form and consisting of five levels. Edzná was first populated c. 400 BCE but was then abandoned c. 1500 CE.

The Tikal National Park in Guatemala contains the ruins of the Mayan city of Tikal, which dominated the region between 200 and 800 CE. "Temple I," shown here, also known as the "Temple of the Great Jaguar," was built c. 695 CE.

Altun Ha, in modern Belize, was a major Mayan ceremonial and trading center between 250 and 900 CE. The "Temple of the Masonry Altars" is the largest of Altun Ha's pyramids, standing at 54 ft (16 m) high.

JAPANESE PYRAMIDS

BELOW

While this appears to be the outline of a classic stepped pyramid of unknown age or origin, it could equally be the result of natural sandstone formations.

Submerged stone structures just below the waters of Yonaguni Jima island at the southern tip of Japan's Ryukyu archipelago remain subject to much debate as to whether they are man-made or a natural geological phenomenon. The largest structure appears to be a stepped pyramid, rising from a depth of 80 ft (25 m).

INDONESIAN PYRAMIDS

"Candi" are Hindi and Buddhist temples built in the main between the 8th and 15th centuries CE. Candi Sukuh in Java is thought to have been built around 1437 CE. It is a simple pyramid fronted by various reliefs and statues, and it was used, along with the other candi in the region, for the worship of ancestors and the observance of fertility rituals.

BELOW
The architecture of Candi Sukuh is reminiscent of Mayan architecture in its stark simplicity.

EUROPEAN PYRAMIDS

Pyramids can be found all over Europe, in countries such as Italy, France, Greece, Spain, and Germany. These pyramids have different forms, serve different functions, and date from different cultures. The relatively recent construction of the glass pyramid at the Louvre in Paris is a testament to our continuing fascination with this geometric form.

ABOVE
The stunning Louvre Pyramid was built in 1989 by the architect I.M. Pei from New York. It is made entirely of glass segments set into a steel skeleton.

RIGHT
The origin of the pyramids at Guimar, on Tenerife, is subject to debate. Some believe that they have links with pre-European Atlantic voyagers.

One of the best preserved ancient buildings in Rome, the pyramid of Cestius was built *c.* 18 BCE as a tomb for the Roman magistrate Gaius Cestius Epulo. It was made from brick-faced concrete covered with slabs of marble.

BELOW
One of the three pyramids of Montevecchia in Italy. These three ancient pyramids were recently captured by satellite image. Initial assessments date the pyramids at over 3,000 years old.

GLOSSARY

cartouche   In archeology "cartouche" generally refers to an oval or oblong that encloses a group of Egyptian hieroglyphs, typically representing the name of a pharaoh.

corbeling   The technique of "corbeling" has been in use since Neolithic times, and involves using rows of corbels (pieces of stone jutting outward) to support any superincumbent weight. It represents a simple form of vaulting and can be seen in many Neolithic chambered cairns. It is also used extensively in Norman and medieval architecture.

capacitor   A device used to store a charge in an electrical circuit. Capacitors function in the same way as batteries, however, the charges and discharges are more efficient, while the amount of charge stored is a great deal less. A simple capacitor is made of two conductors, separated by an insulator, which can be made from paper, plastic, or glass, or can even be a vacuum— in short, any non-conductive material.

conduit   a channel for conveying water or other fluid, for example in a Roman aqueduct. In pyramid research, it is an energy or particle stream beginning at the sun and directed into space.

carbon dating   Discovered in 1949 by Professor Willard Libby of the University of Chicago, this is a technique that uses the naturally occurring isotope carbon-14 to establish the age of archeological artifacts of a biological origin up to about 50,000 years old. When cosmic particles (*see cosmic rays*) collide with atoms in the atmosphere, they create energetic neutrons that in turn collide with nitrogen atoms, creating carbon-14 atoms, which then combine with oxygen to form carbon dioxide. Plants absorb carbon-14 naturally, and as animals and people eat plants they take in carbon-14 as well. Over time, the radioactive carbon-14 is changed into stable (non-radioactive) nitrogen-14. This decay can be used to measure how long ago once-living material died and hence its age.

centrifuge   A motorized assembly that rotates an object around a fixed axis and generates centrifugal forces in gravitational units.

cosmic rays (probes)   Cosmic rays originate in space and enter the Earth's atmosphere in large numbers every day. The term "ray" is incorrect, though widely used, because cosmic particles arrive individually, not in the form of a concentrated beam. Around 90 percent of arriving particles are protons, while 9 percent are helium nuclei (alpha particles), and about 1 percent are electrons. *See carbon dating.* A probe is just the name for the device and equipment that measures the amount of cosmic rays. For example, it could be a Geiger counter or Scintillating counter.

decibel   A unit used to measure the intensity of a sound or the power level of an electrical signal by comparing it with a given level on a logarithmic scale.

ether	In the 19th century, ether was thought to be a hypothetical substance that filled all space in our universe. It would act as a medium that propagated electromagnetic waves (i.e. light, infrared, x-rays, etcetera.) Einstein's Special Theory of Relativity, published in 1905, eliminated the need for an ether and most physicists today do not believe there is such a thing. Many alternative researchers believe that an ether does exist, and new evidence may tend to support it.
electromagnetic spectrum	The entire range of frequencies or wavelengths of electromagnetic radiation, beginning with gamma rays (short wavelength) and extending to long radio waves, including visible light (long wavelength). In pyramid research today, certain frequencies or types of this radiation can be blocked by the energy bubble experimentally produced around pyramids.
gamma rays	A form of electromagnetic radiation produced by sub-atomic particle interactions. They have the highest frequency and the shortest wavelength in the electromagnetic spectrum. Recent studies show that the pyramid energy fields could actually block out this most energetic form of radiation.
harmonic	A series of tones whose vibration frequencies are integral multiples of the fundamental. That is, the frequency of the wave is a whole number multiple of another.
hyperspace	A dimension that is higher than our own. Our space–time world is composed of three spatial dimensions, length, width, and height, and a time dimension.
ions	An atom or molecule that is positively or negatively charged due to losing or gaining electrons.
meteorite	A natural object originating in outer space, composed of rocks, iron, or a combination of the two, that enters the atmosphere and survives an impact with the Earth. Modern classification schemes divide meteorites into groups according to their structure, chemical and isotopic composition, and mineralogy. The three major groups of meteorites are iron, stony, and a combination called stony-iron meteorites.
oscilloscope	A piece of electronic equipment that allows voltages to be viewed as a two-dimensional graph. Used in many areas of science, including archeology, when accurate measurements of voltage or current need to be obtained.
pyramidology	A controversial speculation as to the origin and purpose of the Great Pyramid of Giza. Pyramidologists have suggested, among other things, that the geometric specifications of the Great Pyramid carry some coded message, and even that it was not built by the civilizations attributed to it, but possibly by the ancient patriarchs of the bible, (e.g. Enoch or Seth). They also believe that the Great Pyramid was built with divine inspiration and encodes historical dates in its design.
polyphasic communications	A form of electronic wave generation where each phase of the wave is time independent of all the others.
quantum mechanics	Initially developed to provide a better explanation of the atom and subatomic particles, quantum mechanics is the study of the relationship between energy and matter.

BIBLIOGRAPHY

This bibliography is one of the most extensive references for books about the Great Pyramid and related subjects in English from the 17th century to the present. I would like to thank all the library staff that helped me to find copies of some of these rare and exciting books.

Adams, Marsham, *The Book of the Master of the Hidden Place*, 1933

Alford, A.F., *Pyramid of Secrets: The Architecture of the Great Pyramid Reconsidered in the Light of Creational Mythology*, 2003

Anderson, U.S., *The Secret Power of the Pyramids*, 1977

Archibald, R.C., *The Pyramids and Cosmic Energy*, 1972

Austin, Marshall, *Solved Secrets of the Pyramid of Cheops*, 1976

Aziz, Phillipe, *The Mysteries of the Great Pyramid*, 1977

Ballard, Robert, *The Solution of the Pyramid Problem*, 1882

Bauval, Robert and Gilbert, Adrian, *The Orion Mystery*, 1995

Belzoni, Giovanni B., *Narrative of the Operations and Recent Discoveries within the Pyramids, Temples, Tombs, and Excavations in Egypt and Nubia*, 1822

Benavides, R., *Dramatic Prophesies of the Great Pyramid*, 1970

Bonwick, James, *Pyramid Facts and Fancies*, 1877

Bothwell, A., *The Magic of the Pyramid*, 1915

Brier, Bob, *Ancient Egyptian Magic*, 1980

Brennan, Herbie, *The Secret History of Ancient Egypt*, 2001

Bristowe, E. S. G., *The Man Who Built the Great Pyramid*, 1932

Brooke, M.W.H.L., *The Great Pyramid of Gizeh*, 1908

Brunton, Paul, *A Search in Secret Egypt*, 1936

Budge, Sir Wallis, *The Book of the Dead*, 1994

Budge, Sir Wallis, *Egyptian Magic*, 1971

Burn, James, *History of the Great Pyramid*, 1937

Raymond, Capt. E., *Study in Pyramidology*, 1986

Raymond, Capt. E, *The Great Pyramid Decoded*, 1993

Chapman, Arthur Wood, *The Prophecy of the Pyramid*, 1933

Chapman, Francis W., *The Great Pyramid of Gizeh from the Aspect of Symbolism*, 1931

Chase, J. Munsell, *The Riddle of the Sphinx*, 1915

Clayton, Peter and Price, Martin, *The Seven Wonders of the Ancient World*, 1988

Cole, J. H., *Determination of the Exact Size and Orientation of the Great Pyramid of Giza*, 1925

Cook, Robin, *The Pyramids of Giza*, 1992

Corbin, Bruce, *The Great Pyramid, God's Witness in Stone*, 1935

Cottrell, Leonard, *The Mountains of Pharaoh*, 1956

Davidson, Dan, *Shape Power*, 1997

Davidson, David, *The Great Pyramid, Its Divine Message*, 1928

Davidovits, Joseph and Morris, Margie, *The Pyramids: An Enigma Solved*, 1988

Day, St. John Vincent, *Papers on the Great Pyramid*, 1870

Denon, Dominique Vivant, *Travels in Upper and Lower Egypt*, 1803

Devereux, Paul, *Places of Power: Measuring the Secret Energy of Ancient Sites*, 1999

Dunn, Christopher, *The Giza Power Plant*, 1998

Ebon, Martin, *Mysterious Pyramid Power*, 1976

Edgar, John and Morton, *Pyramid Passages*, 1912-13

Edwards, I.E.S., *The Pyramids of Egypt*, 1949

Eliade, Mircea, *A History of Religious Ideas*, 3 Volumes, 1978

Evans, Humphrey, *The Mystery of the Pyramids*, 1979

Fakhry, Ahmed, *The Pyramids*, 1961

Farrell, Joseph P., *The Giza Death Star*, 2001

Faulkner, Raymond, *The Ancient Egyptian Pyramid Texts*, 1969

Faulkner, Raymond, *The Ancient Egyptian Book of the Dead*, 1996

Fish, Everett W., *Egyptian Pyramids, An Analysis of a Great Mystery*, 1880

Fix, William, *Pyramid Odyssey*, 1978

Flanagan, Pat, *Pyramid Power*, 1973

Flanagan, Pat, *Beyond Pyramid Power*, 1976

Flanagan, Pat, *The Pyramid and Its Relationship to Biocosmic Energy*, 1971

Ford, S. H., *The Great Pyramid of Egypt*, 1882

Gabb, Thomas, *Finis Pyramidis: or, Disquistions concerning the Antiquity and scientific end of the Great Pyramid of Giza, or ancient Memphis, in Egypt*, 1806

Gamier, Col. J., *The Great Pyramid: Its Builder and Its Prophecy*, 1912

Gangstad, John E., *The Great Pyramid: Signs in the Sun*, 1976

Gaunt, Bonnie, *Stonehenge and the Great Pyramid*, 1993

Goose, A.B., *The Magic of the Pyramids*, 1915

Gill, Joseph B., *The Great Pyramid Speaks: An Adventure in Mathematical Archaeology*, 1984

Graham, Edwin R., *The Ancient Days or the Pyramid of Ghizeh in the Light of History*, 1888

Gray, Julian Thorbim, *The Authorship and Message of the Great Pyramid*, 1953

Greaves, John, *Pyramidographia*, 1646

Grinsell, Leslie V., *Egyptian Pyramids*, 1947

Haberman, Fredrick, *The Great Pyramid's Message to America*, 1932

Hall, Manly P., *The Secret Teachings of all Ages*, 1969

Hancock, Graham, *Fingerprints of the Gods*, 1995

Hancock, Graham and Bauval, Robert, *The Message of the Sphinx*, 1996

Hawass, Z., *The Pyramids of Ancient Egypt*, 1990

Holt, Erica, *The Sphinx and the Great Pyramid*, 1968

Hope, Murry, *The Ancient Wisdom of Egypt*, 1998

Horn, Paul, *Inside Paul Horn: The Spiritual Odyssey of a Universal Traveler*, 1990

Horn, Paul, *"Inside the Great Pyramid,"* booklet with LP, 1977

Hurtak, J.J., *The Book of Knowledge: The Keys of Enoch*, 1987

Hutchings, N.W., *The Great Pyramid: Prophecy in Stone*, 1996

James, Sir Henry, *Notes on the Great Pyramid of Egypt and the Cubits used in its Design*, 1860

Johnson, C., *Earth/matrix Science in Ancient Artwork, Series No. 77. The Great Pyramid*, 1996

Jordan, Paul, *Riddles of the Sphinx*, 1998

Keable, Julian, *How the Pyramids Were Built*, 1989

Kerrel, Bill and Goggin, Kathy, *The Guide to Pyramid Energy*, 1975

Kingsland, William, *The Great Pyramid in Fact and in Theory*, 1932

Kinnaman, J.O., *The Great Pyramid*, 1943

Knight, Charles S., *The Mystery and Prophecy of the Great Pyramid*, 1933

Kunkel, Edward J., *Pharaoh's Pump*, 1962

Lawton, Ian and Ogilvie-Herald, Chris, *Giza: The Truth*, 1999

Lehner, Mark, *The Complete Pyramids*, 1997

Lemesurier, Peter, *The Great Pyramid Decoded*, 1997

Lemesurier, Peter, *Decoding the Great Pyramid*, 1999

Lemesurier, Peter, *The Great Pyramid, Your Personal Guide*, 1987

Lemesurier, Peter, *The Stones Cry Out*, 1976

Lepre, J.P., *The Egyptian Pyramids*, 1990

Lewis, David, *Mysteries of the Pyramids*, 1978

Lewis, H. Spencer, *The Symbolic Prophecy of the Great Pyramid*, 1936

Macaulay, David, *Pyramid*, 1975

MacHuisdean, W. Hamish, *The Great Law*, 1924

Malek, Jaromir, *In the Shadow of the Pyramids*, 1986

Mann, Elizabeth, *The Great Pyramid*, 1996

Marks, T. Septimus, *The Great Pyramid, Its History and Teachings*, 1879

Meyler, Stephen S, *The Land of Osiris*, 2001

Nicklein, J. Bernard, *Testimony in Stone*, 1961

Marshall, Austin, *Solved Secrets of the Pyramid of Cheops*, 1976

Massey, Gerald, *Ancient Egypt: The Light of the World*, 1907

McCarty, Louis P., *The Great Pyramid of Jeezeh*, 1907

Mendelssohn, Kurt, *The Riddle of the Pyramids*, 1975

McCollum, Rocky, *The Prime Mover*, 1971

McCollum, Rocky, *The Giza Necropolis Decoded*, 1975

Nelson, Dee Jay and Coville, David, *Life Forces in the Great Pyramid*, 1977

Newton, Sir Isaac, *Principia*, reprint, 1937

Noone, Richard, *5/5/2000 Ice: The Ultimate Disaster*, 1986

Norden, F.L., *Travels in Egypt and Nubia*, 2 Volumes, 1757

Ostrander, S. and L. Schroeder, *Psychic Discoveries Behind the Iron Curtain*, 1970

Owen, A.R.G., *The Shapes of Egyptian Pyramids*, 1973

Papeloux, Gaston, *The Nocturnal Magic of the Pyramids*, 1961

Perring, John Shae, *The Pyramids of Gizeh from Actual Survey and Measurement on the Spot*, 1839-42

Petrie, William Flinders, *The Pyramids and Temples of Gizeh*, 1883

Phillips, John, *The Great Pyramid and its Design*, 1977

Picknett, Lynn and Clive Prince, *The Stargate Conspiracy*, 1999

Pochan, Andre, *The Mysteries of the Great Pyramid*, 1978

Pococke, Richard, *The Travels of Pococke through Egypt*, 1762–90

Proctor, Richard, *The Great Pyramid, Observatory, Tomb, and Temple*, 1883

Rand, Howard B., *The Challenge of the Great Pyramid*, 1943

Randall, Rev. D.A., *The Handwriting of God in Egypt, Sinai, and the Holy Land: The Records of a Journey from the Great Valley of the West to the Sacred Places of the East*, 1862

Rawlinson, G., *History of Herodotus*, 1912

Riffert, George R., *Great Pyramid Proof of God*, 1932

Robinson, Lytle, *The Great Pyramid and Its Builders*, 1966

Rolt-Wheeler, F.W., *The Pyramid Builder*, 1929

Rutherford, Adam, *Pyramidology*, 4 Volumes 1957-1972

Sandys, George, *Sandys Travailes*, 1652

Schul, Bill and Pettit, Ed, *The Secret Power of Pyramids*, 1975

Schul, Bill and Pettit, Ed, *Pyramids and the Second Reality*, 1979

Schwaller de Lubicz, R.A., *The Temple in Man*, 1949

Seiss, Joseph A, *A Miracle in Stone or the Great Pyramid of Egypt*, 1877

Siliotti, Alberto, *Guide to the Pyramids of Egypt*, 1997

Sinett, Alfred P., *The Pyramids and Stonehenge*, 1958

Sitchin, Zecharia, *The Stairway to Heaven*, 1980

Skinner, James Ralston, *Actual Measures of the Great Pyramid*, 1880

Smith, Warren, *The Secret Forces of the Pyramids*, 1975

Smith, Worth, *The Miracle of the Ages*, 1937

Smyth, Charles Piazzi, *Our Inheritance in the Great Pyramid*, 1880

Steiner, Rudolf, *Egyptian Myths and Mysteries*, 1971

Stewart, Basil, *The Great Pyramid: Its Construction, Symbolism, and Chronology*, 1927

Stark, Norman H., *First Practical Pyramid Book*, 1977

Stewart, Basil, *The Mystery of the Great Pyramid*, 1929

Stewart, Basil, *History and Significance of the Great Pyramid*, 1935

Sykes, Egerton, *The Pyramids of Egypt*, 1973

Taylor, John, *The Great Pyramid: Why Was It Built and Who Built it?* 1864

Temple, Robert, *The Sirius Mystery*, 1976

Ronald Temple, *The Message from the King's Coffer*, 1920

Tompkins, Peter, *Secrets of the Great Pyramid*, 1971

Tompkins, Peter, *Mysteries of the Mexican Pyramids*, 1976

Toth, Max and Nielsen, Greg, *Pyramid Prophecies*, 1979

Toth, Max, *Pyramid Power*, 1976

Tracey, Benjamin, *The Pillar of Witness*, 1876

Turbeville, Joseph, *A Glimmer of Light from the Eye of a Giant*, 2000

Valentine, Tom, *The Great Pyramid: Man's Monument to Man*, 1975

Von Daniken, Erich, *The Eyes of the Sphinx*, 1996

Von Daniken, Erich, *Chariots of the Gods*, 1971

Vyse, Richard Howard, *Operations Carried Out on the Pyramids of Gizeh in 1837*, 1840-42

Wake, Staniland C., *The Origin and Significance of the Great Pyramid*, 1882

Watson, C.M., *The Coffer of the Great Pyramid*, 1900

Weeks, John, *The Pyramids*, 1971

West, John Anthony, *Serpent in the Sky*, 1979

West, John Anthony, *The Traveler's Keys to Ancient Egypt*, 1995

Wilson, Colin, *From Atlantis to the Sphinx*, 1996

Wyckoff, James, *Pyramid Energy*, 1976

Yeats, Thomas, *A Dissertation of the Antiquity, Origin and Design of the Principal Pyramids of Egypt*, 1833

RESEARCH ARTICLES

Parr, Joe, "Anomalous Radioactive Variations," Electric Spacecraft Journal, Volume 9 (1993)

Parr, Joe, "Tests Prove Pyramid Affects Gamma Rays," Pyramid Guide Journal, Issues 47–53 (1980–81)

Parr, Joe, "Pyramid Research," Advance Sciences Advisory, Mar–Apr (1985) thru Nov–Dec (1985), July–Aug (1987), and Mar–Apr (1988)

Davidson, Dan, *Shape Power*, Rivas Publishing, 1997

Davidson, Dan, "Dielectrics as Gravity Wave Detectors," Proceedings of the 1991 Extraordinary Science Conference (1991). Also presented at 1992 International Tesla Symposium in Colorado

INDEX

ACKNOWLEDGMENTS

Alexander and Anatoli Golod, my colleagues and good friends, who built the Russian and Ukrainian pyramids. They supplied me with the wonderful photographs of their pyramids and the results of the research that they carried out within them.

Dr. Volodymyr Krasnoholvets, my Ukrainian colleague who first told me about the Russian and Ukrainian pyramids and research. He has always kept me updated and I thank him for his close friendship over the last several years.

Joe Parr, my colleague and dear friend, who supplied me with information, photographs, and results of his research. I will always cherish our hours of conversation and brainstorming sessions. His contribution to the field of pyramid research will have an impact for decades.

Dr. Patrick Flanagan, a legend in pyramid research, who I have admired for most of my life. His pioneering work has been the basis of modern pyramid research. He has been a constant source of inspiration and a very close friend.

Jon Bodsworth, who supplied me with breathtaking photographs of the interior and exterior of the Great Pyramid. His photos are the best I have ever seen of the Great Pyramid and the Giza Plateau.

Dr. J.J. Hurtak, my close friend and colleague, who I thank for his advice and contributions to this book. The additions and suggestions he provided for Appendix 3, Pyramids on Mars, have been invaluable.

Stephen DeSalvo, who helped with the editing of this book, and provided many great ideas and suggestions.

Chris DeSalvo, for his creative contributions to this book and his constant encouragement.

John Anthony West, whose pioneering research has changed the world of Egyptology. I am grateful for his friendship and the wonderful conversations that I have had with him through the years.

Robert Bauval, whose books have stimulated new ideas and research regarding the Great Pyramid of Giza.

Paul Horn, our first Honorary Advisory Board Member, for his promotion of the Great Pyramid through his album *Inside the Great Pyramid*.

PETER TOMPKINS, author of *Secrets of the Great Pyramid*, who has probably done the most to promote interest in the Great Pyramid.

PAUL MALONEY, archeology colleague and one of my closest friends for over thirty years.

RUDOLF GANTENBRINK for permission to use several of his wonderful photographs of his exploration of the airshafts at the Great Pyramid.

NANCY LAVIGNA, my mother-in-law, who actually read the first draft of my manuscript and constantly gave me encouragement and support.

DAN AND NANCY SCHMIDT, the greatest friends anyone could have.

BOB REISNER, a dear friend who has given me good advice for many years.

THE ADVISORY BOARD OF THE GREAT PYRAMID OF GIZA RESEARCH ASSOCIATION, including Dr. J. J. Hurtak, Dr. Patrick Flanagan, Christopher Dunn, Stephen Meyler, Andres Washington, Dennis Balthaser, Jeff Rense, Dan Davidson, Bernard Pietsch, John Cadman, Dr. George Bayer, David Salmon, Serguey and Svetlana Gorbunova, and many others for their kind friendship and research contributions.

To the wonderful STAFF AT IVY, including the Editorial Director, Caroline Earle, the very talented Art Director, Sarah Howerd, and my Editor, Mary Todd, who worked day and night with her colleagues to make this book the best it could be. No author could ask for a more creative, competent, and brilliant staff. I have made new friends and I thank them for their support.

I would like especially to acknowledge my literary agent, DAVID ALEXANDER, who always believed in this project. Even when I lost faith, he never gave up. I am eternally grateful to him for his efforts in making this book happen.

To my wife VALERIE whose constant support and encouragement made this possible.

And to my wonderful children, CHRISTOPHER, STEPHEN, PAUL, and VERONICA, who also gave me great encouragement and help with the writing of this book.

In memory of my dear parents, JOHN AND ANNA DESALVO, who tolerated and even encouraged my scientific curiosity.

And finally, to the GREAT PYRAMID OF GIZA— still the first wonder of the world.

PICTURE CREDITS

The publishers would like to thank the following for permission to use images.

AKG IMAGES
4R (Bildarchiv Steffens), 7 (Bildarchiv Steffens), 14B (Andrea Jemolo), 26L, 26R (Bildarchiv Steffens), 33T (Hervé Champollion), 35 (Alfio Garozzo), 42B (Erich Lessing), 46, 47T (Erich Lessing), 49, 50T (Andrea Jemolo), 52B (James Morris), 54 (Erich Lessing), 62R (Electa), 62L (Electa), 63T (Erich Lessing), 64 (Visioars), 79 (Erich Lessing), 81T (Erich Lessing), 85 (Bildarchiv Steffens), 86TL (Andrea Jemolo), 88B (Rabatti-Domingie), 90T (Erich Lessing), 91T (Bildarchiv Steffens), 91B (Nimatallah), 92L, 100TR (Cameraphoto), 140T (Alfons Rath), 151 (Gilles Mermet), 158, 167 (Tristan Lafranchis), 168T (Andrea Jemolo), 168B (François Guénet), 171T (Veintimilla), 177T (Tristan Lafranchis), 186.

ANCIENT ART AND ARCHITECTURE COLLECTION
23 (J. Stevens), 86BR (R.Sheridan), 180 (J.Stevens).

THE ART ARCHIVE
18B (Bibliothèque des Arts Décoratifs Paris/Gianni Dagli Orti).

JOHN BODSWORTH
21, 25T, 25B, 27L, 32T, 32B, 37, 38, 70, 72.

BRIDGEMAN ART LIBRARY
8 (Giraudon), 31L (Private Collection/ The Stapleton Collection), 71B (Private Collection/The Stapleton Collection), 71T (Stapleton Collection, UK), 75T (Harris Museum and Art Gallery, Preston, Lancashire, UK), 83T (Louvre, Paris, France/Giraudon), 87 (Giraudon), 89BL (Egyptian National Museum, Cairo, Egypt/Photo © Held Collection), 89T (Victoria & Albert Museum, London, UK), 117B (Private Collection/Archives Charmet), 117T (Private Collection/The Stapleton Collection), 129T (Ken Welsh), 169T (Bildarchiv Steffens).

MARCO BUSONI
137B, 177B.

MARTIN CHILLMAID
119T.

CORBIS
Front Cover (Jean-Pierre Lescourret), Back Cover (Roger Wood), 1 (Chris Rainer), 2 (Chris Rainer), 5 (Kazuyoshi Nomachi), 10 (Kazuyoshi Nomachi), 11 (Jean-Pierre Lescourret), 13 (Chris Rainer), 14T (Roger Ressmeyer), 16T (Roger Wood), 18T (Sean Sexton Collection), 20 (Yann Arthus-Bertrand), 44B (Reuters), 45B (Patrick Robert/ Sygma), 53T (Bettmann), 57 (Roger Ressmeyer), 61B (Bettmann), 61T (Christie's Images), 62T (Bettmann), 63B (Wolfgang Kaehler), 65B (Bettmann), 66B, 69 (Randy Faris), 76 (Bettmann), 81 (Roger Ressmeyer), 86BL (Gianni Dagli Orti), 89BR (The Art Archive), 92R (Michele Westmorland), 93 (Bernard Annebicque), 95 (Roger Ressmeyer), 97 (V. Velengurin/RPG/Sygma), 98T (V. Velengurin/RPG/Sygma), 98B (V. Velengurin/RPG/Sygma), 99 (V. Velengurin/RPG/Sygma), 100BL (V. Velengurin/RPG/Sygma), 101TL (V. Velengurin/RPG/Sygma), 105 (V. Velengurin/RPG/Sygma, 107B (Ken Kaminesky/Take 2 Productions), 108 (V. Velengurin/RPG/Sygma), 110T (Visuals Unlimited), 111BR (Clouds Hill Imaging Ltd), 113 (Yann Arthus-Bertrand), 115T (V. Velengurin/RPG/Sygma), 121 (Andrew Unangst), 123B (Bryan Allan), 129B (Jonathan Blair), 130 (Guenter Rossenbach/zefa), 134T (Beauchamp Jaques/Sygma), 141T (Bertrand Rieger/Hemis), 144T (Kazuyoshi Nomachi), 149 (Bettmann), 152 (Kazuyoshi Nomachi), 153 (Roger Wood), 155 (Larry Lee Photography), 156 (Roger Wood), 161 (Roger Ressmeyer), 172T (Michele Westmorland), 173B (Buddy Mays), 176T (Bernard Annebicque), 184 (Chris Rainer), 185 (Andrew Unangst), 188 (Yann Arthus-Bertrand), 190 (Chris Rainer).

JOHN AND MORTON EDGAR
33B, 39T, 39B, 42T, 43, 77B.

EGYPTIAN HEALING RODS LTD
135.

DR. PATRICK FLANAGAN
134B, 163.

DR. JOANN FLETCHER
17T, 52T.

RUDOLF GANTENBRINK
44T, 45T, 47B.

GETTY IMAGES
Inside font cover (John Chard), 4L (Will & Deni McIntyre), 75B (Hulton Archive), Frank Greenaway/DK (131M), 141B, 142T (AFP), 143 (Time & Life Pictures), 146 (John Chard), 169B (Sylvain Grandada), 141B (Time & Life Pictures).

ANATOLI GOLOD
94, 101BR, 102B, 103T, 110TL, 110BL, 189.

DR. DESIREE HURTAK-LUIZ C.
82.

iSTOCKPHOTO
145M (Dave Rodriguez).

JUPITER IMAGES
140B, 157B.

MARY EVANS PICTURE LIBRARY
29, 77T, 142B.

NASA
103B, 118B, 127 (UCLA/MIT/ M.Muno et al.), 148, 164T, 164B, 165T, 165B.

OSHO INTERNATIONAL
133, 136, 137T.

PA PHOTOS/AP
17B.

JOE PARR
122, 123T, 124.

PHOTOSHOT
110BR (UPPA), 119B (UPPA).

REX FEATURES
125B (Denis Cameron), 139 (Sipa), 175 (Jane Sweeney/Robert Harding)

COURTESY OF ROBERT M. SCHOCH (©)
174.

SCIENCE PHOTO LIBRARY
66T (David Parker), 106 (Alfred Pasieka), 107 (Custom Medical Stock Photo).

TOPFOTO
30 (World History Archive), 59 (Artmedia/HIP), 60 (Heaton), 65T (Kike Calvo), 67T, 67B (Imageworks), 75B (Photri), 80 (Charles Walker), 90B (Charles Walker), 102T (RIA Novosti), 109 (Imageworks), 116 (RIA Novosti), 118T (Keystone), 131T (Alinari), 131B (World History Archive), 144B (Alinari), 145T (World History Archive), 157T, 159 (John Hedgecoe), 170B (Charles Walker), 170T (Imageworks), 172B (Dallas & John Heaton), 173T (Imageworks), 176B (Dave Walsh), 187 (Aartmedia/HIP).

VOLODYMYR KRASNOHOLOVETS
114BL, 114BR.

WERNER FORMAN ARCHIVE
16B (The Egyptian Museum, Cairo), 19 (British Museum, London), 34 (Schimmel Collection, New York), 41, 50B (The Egyptian Museum, Cairo), 51 (Ny Carlsberg Glyptotek, Copenhagen), 53B, 55, 56, 83B, 88T (The Louvre, Paris), 145B (Fitzwilliam Museum, Cambridge), 182.

Every effort has been made to contact copyright holders, however we apologize if there are any unintentional ommissions.